Designed For Success

Off-Road Vehicles

Revised & Updated

Heinemann
LIBRARY

Ian Graham

www.heinemann.co.uk/library
Visit our website to find out more information about **Heinemann Library** books.

To order:
☎ Phone 44 (0) 1865 888066
▤ Send a fax to 44 (0) 1865 314091
▣ Visit the Heinemann Bookshop at www.heinemann.co.uk/library to browse our catalogue and order online.

First published in Great Britain by Heinemann Library, Halley Court, Jordan Hill, Oxford, OX2 8EJ, part of Harcourt Education. Heinemann is a registered trademark of Harcourt Education Ltd.

© Harcourt Education Ltd 2008
The moral right of the proprietor has been asserted.

Editorial: Andrew Farrow and Dan Nunn
Design: Steven Mead and Geoff Ward
Illustrations: Geoff Ward
Picture Research: Melissa Allison
Production: Alison Parsons

Originated by Modern Age
Printed and bound in China by South China Printing Company

ISBN 978 0 431 16580 6 (hardback)
13 12 11 10 09 08
10 9 8 7 6 5 4 3 2 1

ISBN 978 0 431 16588 2 (paperback)
13 12 11 10 09 08
10 9 8 7 6 5 4 3 2 1

British Library Cataloguing-in-Publication Data
Graham, Ian, 1953 –
    Off-road vehicles. -– (Designed for success) 2nd edition
    1. Off-road vehicles – Juvenile literature
    I. Title
    629.2'2042
A full catalogue record for this book is available from the British Library.

Acknowledgements
The publishers would like to thank the following for permission to reproduce photographs:
© Alvey & Towers pp. **10**, **11** (top), **11** (middle), **11** (bottom), **25** (bottom); © Auto Express pp. **4**, **7** (top), **9** (middle), **12**, **16**, **17**, **18** (left), **24** (bottom), contents; © British Motor Industry Heritage Trust pp. **7** (bottom), **29**; © Camera Press/Susan Goldman p. **6** (bottom); © Corbis pp. **3**, **14**, **15**, **22**; © Corbis/Reuters/Wolfgang Rattay p. **25** (top); © Dutton Maritime Ltd pp. **21** (middle), **21** (bottom); © European Press Agency/PA Photos p. **6** (top); © Holden p. **5** (top); © Jeep World p. **20**; © Land Rover Press Office pp. **5** (bottom), **9** (bottom); © MPL p. **23** (bottom); © National Motor Museum p. **23** (top); © Nick Dimbleby pp. **1**, **9** (top), **12**, **18** (right); © NMM/Dunlop p. **24** (top); © Octagon p. **26**; © PA Photos/Barry Batchelor p. **21** (top); © Ragnar Roberts p. **27** (top); © Superstock p. **28**; © Tografox/R.D. Battersby pp. **13**, **27** (bottom).

Cover photograph reproduced with permission of © Superstock/age fotostock. Background images by © istockphoto/Jan Rihak and © Corbis.

Every effort has been made to contact copyright holders of any material reproduced in this book. Any omissions will be rectified in subsequent printings if notice is given to the publishers.

Disclaimer
All the Internet addresses (URLs) given in this book were valid at the time of going to press. However, due to the dynamic nature of the Internet, some addresses may have changed, or sites may have ceased to exist since publication. While the author and publishers regret any inconvenience this may cause readers, no responsibility for any such changes can be accepted by either the author or the publishers.

Jackaroo ▷

Sometimes the same vehicle is made in different countries under different names. A manufacturer in one country may build its own vehicle using a successful **chassis** (frame) and engine designed by another manufacturer in another country. A "jackaroo" is the name given to a trainee on an Australian sheep or cattle station. It's also an off-road vehicle produced by the Australian car-maker Holden until 2003. Under its Holden bodywork, the Jackaroo was based on the successful Japanese Isuzu Trooper.

All-round rover ▽

Land Rover's Range Rover was introduced in 1970. It made ORVs fashionable. As well as performing well off-road, it could carry heavy loads, and was comfortable enough to be used as a family car. It made many people who never drove off-road want to own an ORV.

The Range Rover is designed to be equally at home on-road or off-road.

Rugged design

An off-road vehicle designer starts with a list of the challenges the vehicle has to deal with. The designer then works out a solution for each problem.

When a normal car crosses rough ground, it risks crashing down onto a rock and smashing itself. The first thing a designer does is to raise the vehicle higher so that there is more **ground clearance**. The bottom of the vehicle may also be protected by a thick metal plate. To give the maximum grip, all four wheels are driven by the engine, instead of just two. To give even more grip on soft or loose surfaces, the tyres are more deeply grooved than normal car tyres. An ORV's rugged construction enables it to keep going on uneven, rocky, or slippery ground without bending or breaking.

The Hummer ▷

The High-Mobility Multipurpose Wheeled Vehicle (HMMWV) is perhaps the ultimate off-road vehicle. It is known as a "Humvee" or "Hummer". It was designed as a **military** replacement for the Jeep, so it can cope with the toughest conditions. The driver can let the tyres down or **inflate** them at the press of a switch while the vehicle is still moving. Letting out some air makes the tyres squash down and spread out so that they grip soft ground better.

◁ Civilian Hummer

The **civilian** version of the Hummer is about half a metre wider than most other off-roaders. Its extra width makes it more difficult to tip over. It can climb steeper slopes than other mass-produced ORVs.

◁ On the farm

Tractors are designed specifically for working off-road. They have to cope with all sorts of surfaces, often while pulling a heavy trailer or machine. Their big wheels give a smoother ride over rough ground or ploughed fields. The special tyres have thick rubber bars sticking out. They're designed like this so that the bars dig into soft ground and stop the wheels from spinning or sinking.

GENERAL MOTORS "HUMMER" H2

Engine: 6.0-litre V8

Engine power: 329 hp

Length: 5.2 metres

Weight: 2,903 kg

Top speed: 160 kph (99 mph)

Out of trouble ▽

Working ORVs like this early Land Rover are often equipped with a **winch**. An off-roader with a winch can pull itself out of trouble. The cable is pulled out and anchored to a tree. Then the winch can wind the cable in and drag the vehicle out of difficulty.

The secret behind an ORV's **performance**, especially in the most extreme conditions, is the way its engine drives the wheels.

It may seem surprising, but a car's wheels often spin at different speeds! When a car turns, the wheels on the outside of the bend travel further than the wheels on the inside. And the front wheels (used to steer) travel further than the rear wheels. The car has a device called a **differential**. The differential lets a wheel on one side spin faster than a wheel on the other side. It works well for a family car, but is disastrous for an ORV. If one wheel grips the ground, but the wheel on the other side slips, the differential lets all the engine power go to the slipping wheel. One wheel stops, the other spins wildly. So, ORV designers have found a way of letting the wheels spin at different speeds on normal roads, but locking them together on soft ground.

Different paths ▽

When a normal car turns a corner, its wheels follow slightly different paths along the road. A set of **gearwheels** called a differential is fitted between the two wheels that are driven by the engine. The differential shares out the engine power to the wheels according to how much they need, so that they can turn at different speeds if they need to.

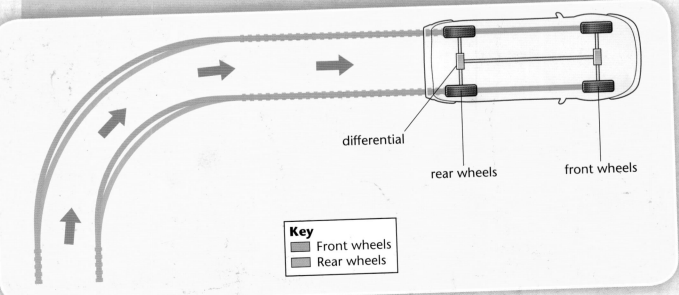

differential

rear wheels

front wheels

Key
- ▬ Front wheels
- ▬ Rear wheels

A slippery problem △

The type of differential used in family cars does not work well for off-road driving. When one wheel of an ORV slips and spins on slippery ground, a normal differential would send all the engine power to that wheel and none to the wheel that is gripping the ground. This means the vehicle would stop dead! One answer is to redesign the differential so that the wheels are allowed to have only a small difference in speed between them. This is known as a "limited slip differential". If one wheel loses grip, this system stops it from spinning wildly. Meanwhile the gripping wheel drives the ORV out of trouble.

Sharing power ▽

All four of an ORV's wheels can be driven by the engine, instead of just two. This is called **four-wheel drive (4x4)**. There is one differential between the front wheels and another differential between the rear wheels.

- The front and rear wheels can be linked so that half of the engine power goes to the front wheels and half to the rear wheels.

- Or, they can be linked by a differential so that each of the four wheels receives as much engine power as it needs.

The Range Rover was the first 4x4 with electronic traction control. It automatically applied the brakes to any of the wheels that slipped.

Quads

Off-road vehicles come in a range of shapes and sizes. The smallest are **four-wheel drive**, sit-on motors called **quads**.

Quads are four-wheel all-terrain vehicles (ATVs). They are designed to be go-anywhere off-roaders for one person. They are used for fun, sport, and work, and they are easier to ride than a motorcycle. The rider sits on top and steers by turning the handlebars. Speed is controlled with either a thumb-activated lever on the handlebars or a **twist-grip**, alongside a foot-operated **gearshift**. They have to have good **suspension** to let the wheels follow all the bumps and holes in the ground without bouncing the rider off. Quads are very stable little vehicles, because the rider sits in the middle of the four wheels. Their built-in stability means that the rider doesn't have to balance as the vehicle motors over rough ground.

◁ Working quads

The Honda FourTrax Foreman 4X4 is a typical modern quad. It's designed to be a hard-working vehicle. Racks on the front and behind the rider can carry cargo. Bigger loads can be hauled in a trailer. Quads like this are called utility vehicles. There are also sport models, designed for speed and **performance** instead of rugged pulling power.

FOURTRAX FOREMAN 4X4

Engine: 475 cc

Length: 2.1 metres

Weight: 270 kg

Kids' quads ▷

Quads are so easy to ride that some models are designed specially for under-16s. They have smaller engines to make them lighter and easier to handle. A youth quad might have a 90**cc** engine, compared to a full-size quad for an adult rider with an engine of 230cc to 500cc. A smaller youth model might weigh just over 100 kilograms, about half the weight of a full-size model.

A quad's design, like this child's version, makes it as easy to service and repair as a motorcycle.

Round 'em up! ▽

A quad's small size, rugged design, and ease of use make it ideal for farmers to get round their fields and visit their animals. They are used to take food to animals in winter, to round up sheep for shearing, and to carry tools and materials around farms and forests. Many of these jobs used to be done on horseback or by means of larger ORVs. Now, they can be done faster, more easily, and less expensively by quads.

Jeep Wrangler

DESIGNING THE BEST

The Jeep Wrangler is designed to cope easily with all conditions, from swamp to sand and everything in between. Its high **ground clearance** of 22 centimetres lets it cross stony or deeply rutted ground without getting caught up on rocks. It can climb steeply and its **suspension** lets the wheels travel up and down so far that it can drive over boulders or fallen trees that would trap most other vehicles, even other off-roaders. Its interior is designed to be equally practical. The carpets can be taken out, the seats are covered with water-resistant material, and there are drain holes in the floor so that mud and dirt can be washed out. The back seat folds down to create enough storage space for camping equipment or fishing gear.

Without power steering, it would be very difficult to handle the Wrangler in tough conditions like this.

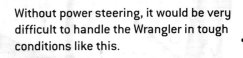

Power steering

It takes a lot of muscle power to turn an ORV's wheels, especially on soft ground. To make it easier, off-roaders like the Wrangler often have power-assisted steering. When the driver turns the steering wheel, a pump forces oil through a pipe – this oil pressure then turns the wheels. The pump and oil magnify the driver's muscle-power and make it easier to steer the vehicle.

JEEP WRANGLER	
Engine: 3.8-litre V-6	
Engine power: 202 hp	
Length: 4.1 metres	
Weight: 1,715 kg	
Top speed: 180 kph (112 mph)	

Springs and things

An ORV designer can choose from two different types of suspension, the springy connection between the vehicle and its wheels.

- Independent suspension lets the wheels move up and down separately. Racing cars use independent suspension. However, loading a vehicle with extra weight makes its **axles** settle lower, making it more likely to hit rocks.

- A different type of suspension, called live axle suspension, keeps the axles and **differentials** at the same height above the ground, no matter how heavily the vehicle is loaded. Working vehicles like the Wrangler use live axle suspension.

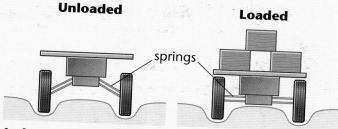

Unloaded **Loaded**

springs

Independent suspension
When the vehicle is loaded up (right), the springs are pressed down and the vehicle settles lower, closer to the ground.

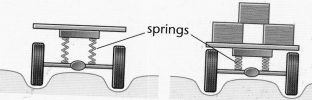

springs

Live axle suspension
The axle is fixed to the **chassis**. The springs fit between the car's body and the chassis. So, when the vehicle is loaded up, compressing the springs, the axle stays at the same height above the ground – good for off-road vehicles.

Leaves and coils

Designers are always on the lookout for better ways of building vehicles.

- The first Jeeps had a suspension system made from leaf **springs**. A leaf spring is made from a pile of thin metal strips bent into a curved shape. It is simple and it works, but there are other types of springs that are even better.

- In 1997, the Wrangler's leaf springs were replaced by coil springs, seen in the middle of this photo. Coil springs let the wheels move a greater distance up and down, which makes the new Wrangler more comfortable to travel in.

CLOSER LOOK

Jeep Wrangler
BUILT FOR HARD KNOCKS

Mass-produced ORVs like the Jeep Wrangler are built on an **assembly line**. Assembly begins with the vehicle's chassis. The Wrangler's chassis is a strong metal frame shaped like a ladder. As the chassis moves along the assembly line, the body, engine, suspension, seats, wheels, and all the other parts are added to it until a complete Wrangler is driven off the end of the line.

This sounds simple, but the assembly line has to be designed with as much care as the vehicles that are built on it. It has to move the vehicles along at precisely the right speed. There has to be enough space around it to store the parts needed for each stage of construction. There have to be powered **hoists** to hold and move heavy parts such as engines. And it has to be well lit and a safe place to work.

Pressing metal

The large metal panels that make the body of the Wrangler are shaped by a method called pressing. To make a door panel, for example, a flat sheet of metal is placed between two metal blocks shaped like the finished panel. On one block, called the punch, the shape of the panel stands out from the surface of the block. The other block, called the die, is hollowed out in the same shape. The punch presses the metal sheet into the hollowed-out die. (Imagine pushing a fist into a cupped hand with a sheet of paper in between them.) The thin metal sheet bends into the shape of the panel.

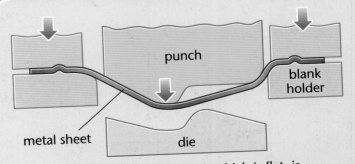

A blank sheet of metal, which is flat, is pressed into the shape of panel needed.

Booting up

An off-roader's tyres are made from a mixture of materials designed to hold air inside, support the vehicle's weight, and transfer its engine power to the ground.

- Rubber is used because it is flexible, airtight, and grips the road.
- Steel hoops embedded in the rubber hold the tyre firmly on the wheel rim.
- Strips of tough material (called body plies) laid from side to side give the tyre its strength.
- Grooves are moulded into the flattened rubber edge of the tyre, called the tread. In wet conditions, the tread helps to squeeze water out from under the tyre.

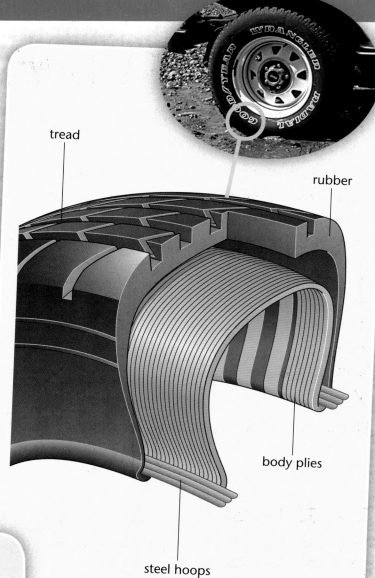

tread

rubber

body plies

steel hoops

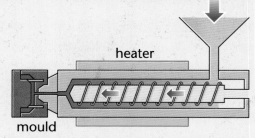

plastic powder/granules in

heater

mould

Melted plastic is forced into the mould.

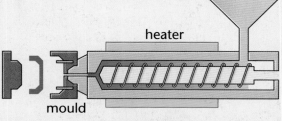

heater

mould

When the plastic has cooled, the mould is opened and the part is removed.

Giving injections

Many of a vehicle's plastic parts are made by a method called "injection moulding". It works by heating plastic powder or granules until they melt. The liquid plastic is then forced into a mould. The plastic fills the mould and takes on its shape. When the plastic cools, it changes from liquid to solid. Finally, the mould is opened and the part is taken out.

CLOSER LOOK

Jeep Wrangler
HARD DRIVING

The Wrangler, and every other Jeep, is designed to be able to drive the Rubicon Trail. This winding, rocky trail is famous amongst off-road drivers. It is the ultimate test of an off-road vehicle's **performance**. It stretches from Loon Lake to Lake Tahoe in northern California, USA, and takes two or three days to complete. Parts of it are strewn with boulders the size of houses!

The Wrangler's small size and its ability to turn tightly let it get round big boulders. These same features make it just as easy to manoeuvre in city traffic and park in small spaces. The Wrangler's 3.8-litre engine is designed to supply plenty of power for off-road work. On-road it can **accelerate** from 0–100 kph (60 mph) in only 9.4 seconds and reach a top speed of 180 kph (112 mph) – that's faster than many family cars.

Two wheels or four?

Four-wheel drive is a must for off-road driving, but it is not necessary for driving on roads. The Jeep Wrangler has part-time four-wheel drive. This means the driver can choose whether to use two-wheel or four-wheel drive. And what is more, the driver can switch between the two while the vehicle is moving. This is called changing "on the fly".

The Wrangler looks as if it has two gear-changing levers. The lever on the right is indeed a gear lever. The lever on the left is used to switch between two-wheel drive and four-wheel drive.

Torque talk

The Wrangler has a 202-**horsepower** engine, but for off-road vehicle designers a second figure is just as important. It is called "torque". A vehicle will not move unless its engine applies a force to turn the wheels. This turning force is called torque. An ORV standing in mud needs more torque to start its wheels moving than a car sitting on a flat, hard road. In fact, the Wrangler's engine produces as much torque as some high-performance sports cars.

Computerized brakes

Like many vehicles, the Jeep Wrangler is fitted with a computerized system called ABS (anti-lock braking system). This lets it stop without skidding, no matter how hard the driver presses the brake pedal. ABS senses the speed of each wheel. If a wheel locks (stops turning) and starts to skid, the brakes are automatically released and then re-applied. The vehicle comes to a halt steadily, without skidding. ORVs also use ABS to stop the wheels from spinning when they lose grip on a slippery surface.

On a normal road surface

Off-road vehicle wheel sitting on hard ground.

small torque needed to start the wheel moving

wheel turns easily on a hard surface

Off-road

Off-road vehicle wheel in soft mud.

more torque needed to overcome the mud's resistance and start the wheel turning

mud makes the wheel more difficult to turn

ABS can stop wheels from spinning in very wet conditions.

A sensor in each wheel sends electronic signals along wires (red) to a control box. If a wheel spins too fast, the control box operates the brake on that wheel to slow it down.

ABS control box

CLOSER LOOK

Engine power

Off-road vehicles are powered by a variety of different engines, from tiny **two-strokes** to massive **diesels**. The designer chooses the engine to suit the size and weight of the vehicle and what it will be used for.

Two-stroke engines power the smallest **quads** and snowmobiles. They are small, simple engines, but they wear out faster than other engines and they produce more air pollution. Larger vehicles are powered by **four-stroke engines**. There are two types, designed to burn different fuels. The simplest and most rugged is the diesel engine. The rest are powered by petrol engines. Whatever the engine type, they all work by burning fuel to push a **piston** down inside a **cylinder**. The up-and-down motion of the piston, or pistons, turns the vehicle's wheels.

A four-stroke petrol engine needs a battery to make the electric sparks that **ignite** the fuel and a radiator to cool the water that flows around the engine.

battery

radiator

ORVs have enormous engine power, not only for driving in difficult conditions, but also for operating equipment, such as **winches**. A winch can be used to pull a vehicle out of trouble if it gets stuck in particularly heavy mud.

Four-stroke

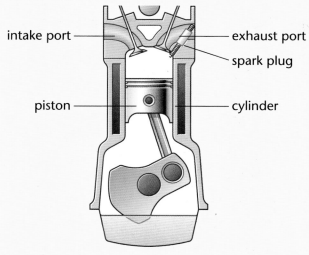

intake port
exhaust port
spark plug
piston
cylinder

Two-stroke

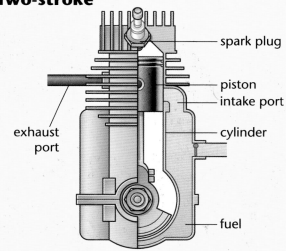

spark plug
piston
intake port
cylinder
exhaust port
fuel

Diesel

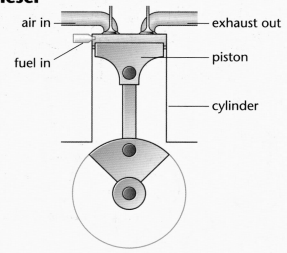

air in
exhaust out
fuel in
piston
cylinder

◁ Four-stroke

Many ORVs are powered by four-stroke petrol engines. Each of the four "strokes" is an up or down movement of one of the engine's pistons inside a cylinder. As the piston moves down the cylinder, it sucks air in through the intake port. Fuel is sprayed into the air. The piston moves up and squashes the air. An electric spark from the spark plug ignites the fuel. The burning fuel heats the air, which pushes the piston down the cylinder. As it rises again, it pushes the burned gases out through the **exhaust** port.

◁ Two-stroke

When a spark ignites the fuel in a two-stroke engine, the piston is forced down the cylinder. On its way, it uncovers a pipe called the exhaust port and the hot gases rush out through it. The piston continues moving down until it uncovers a second pipe called the intake port. A fresh supply of fuel and air rush into the cylinder, the piston rises, and the cycle begins all over again.

◁ Diesel

A diesel engine does not use an electric spark to ignite its fuel. When a piston squashes the air inside a cylinder, the air gets hotter and hotter. As soon as the fuel is sprayed into the cylinder, the air is so hot that the fuel ignites by itself. The air is squashed so much that the engine has to be made very strong to stop it from bursting apart. Because of this, diesel engines are bigger and heavier than petrol engines.

Amphibious cars

Off-road vehicles can drive easily through a few centimetres of water, but an **amphibious** vehicle can be driven straight into the deepest river, lake, or even the sea, because it floats.

Amphibious vehicles work like normal cars on a road and like motorboats in water. To make a car behave like a motorboat, it has to be designed like a motorboat. A motorboat needs a watertight **hull** to stop water leaking inside, so an amphibious car needs a watertight body, too. A motorboat needs a way of propelling itself through the water and so does an amphibious vehicle. The simplest way to move an amphibious car through water is to let its wheels do the work. Knobbly, off-road tyres spinning underwater can move a floating car along at walking pace. To go faster, or to cope with stronger water currents, the car needs a **propeller** to push it through the water.

Jeep-boat ▽

Most of the hundred or so different amphibious vehicles built so far have been **military**. One of the first was based on the famous Second World War Jeep. It was called the Ford GPA "Seep". In water it was powered by a propeller driven by the Jeep's engine. The Seep was intended to ferry troops from ships to the shore. About 5,000 of them were built.

◁ The one and only Amphicar

The only **civilian** amphibious car that ever went into mass production was the Amphicar. About 3,500 of them were produced in the 1960s. It used parts from several other cars – including Mercedes brakes and **suspension**, Porsche **transmission**, and a Triumph Herald engine. Its body was made from steel. In the water, it was powered by propellers driven by the engine. It was steered simply by turning the front wheels.

Mariner ▷

The Dutton Commander is a modern amphibious car. The body is made from **GRP (glass reinforced plastic)**, because, unlike steel, GRP does not rust. In water, it is powered by a **water-jet** from a 20-centimetre propeller. In 2006, two Dutton amphibious cars crossed the English Channel in just over seven hours.

DUTTON COMMANDER AMPHIBIOUS CAR

Engine: 1.3 litres

Engine power: 85 hp

Length: 4.72 metres

Weight: 1150 kg

Speed in water: 10 kph (6 mph)

Dune buggies

Most off-road vehicles are designed to do a job, but dune buggies, or sandrails, are recreational vehicles — they're for having fun. These skeleton-like cars are designed for thrilling, fast drives on sand.

A dune buggy begins as a frame made from steel tubes welded together. The engine is usually placed at the back, where its weight helps press the big rear tyres down into the sand to get more grip. A Volkswagen 1,600**cc** or 2-litre engine is a popular choice. Most dune buggies are two-seaters, but by lengthening the frame, two more passenger seats can be fitted in. The majority of dune buggies are one-offs built by their owners. But they are now so popular, especially in the USA, that manufacturers have started to produce kits of parts and even complete cars.

Leaping off sand dunes is all part of the fun of driving a dune buggy.

Safety first ▽

The most important part of a dune buggy is its roll bar or roll cage — a high bar or metal frame that loops over above the driver's head. If the buggy gets flipped over and lands upside down, the roll bar or cage is designed to support the car's weight and stop the people inside from being crushed.

◁ Sand blasters

People started having off-road fun with the Beach Buggy in the early 1960s. The dune buggies being built at that time were heavy and cumbersome. Then boat designer Bruce Meyers used his knowledge of building lightweight **fibre-glass** boats to redesign the dune buggy. He put a fibre-glass body on a shortened, rear-engined Volkswagen **chassis**. The result was an off-roader that was light, fast, and great fun. Thousands of Beach Buggies were sold in kit form for people to build themselves.

Military buggies ▽

Special forces often operate in small groups travelling fast and light. They race ahead of troops to scout out the land ahead, spy on enemy forces, and strike wherever they can. Normal **military** ORVs are too big for their needs. Dune buggies are perfect. Military dune buggies, or "fast attack vehicles", must be reliable — because a breakdown could leave troops stranded in enemy territory. For use in the desert, a good air filter is also essential. It stops sand from being sucked into the engine and damaging it.

Snow vehicles ▷

In some countries, the roads become covered in snow and ice every year, so even "on-road vehicles" have to cope with off-road conditions.

Snow and ice are especially difficult to drive on, even in an off-road vehicle, because they are so slippery. A vehicle has to be able to grip the surface in order to **accelerate**, brake, and steer. Without grip, it can't do any of these things. One answer is to fit a standard ORV with tyres designed to bite into slippery ground. Extra-chunky winter tyres can deal with snow and ice on normal roads, but thick ice needs a different design solution – studded tyres. They are covered with hundreds of steel studs or spikes that bite into the ice.

Really deep snow is too much for any normal off-roader, even one fitted with studded tyres. These extreme conditions need a whole new vehicle specially designed for the purpose – the answer is the snowmobile!

Studs: good or bad? ▷

Studded tyres give ORVs grip on ice, but they can damage roads. In Norway, about 250,000 tonnes of **asphalt** is worn off the roads every year by studded tyres. Repairing this damage is very expensive. It is also bad for the environment and perhaps for people, too. Some of the dust produced by stud damage is blown up into the air, adding to air pollution, and some of it is breathed in by people.

Four-wheel drive is essential for driving on snow and ice, because all four wheels grip the slippery surface. A family car is more likely to slip and slide, because only two wheels grip the ground.

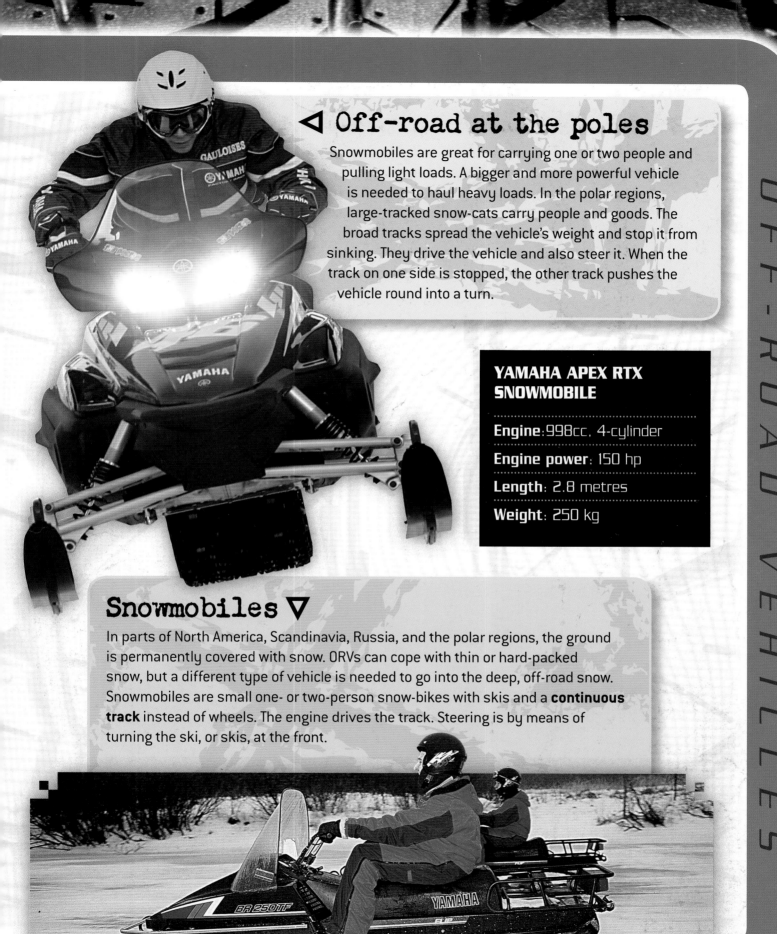

◁ Off-road at the poles

Snowmobiles are great for carrying one or two people and pulling light loads. A bigger and more powerful vehicle is needed to haul heavy loads. In the polar regions, large-tracked snow-cats carry people and goods. The broad tracks spread the vehicle's weight and stop it from sinking. They drive the vehicle and also steer it. When the track on one side is stopped, the other track pushes the vehicle round into a turn.

YAMAHA APEX RTX SNOWMOBILE

Engine: 998cc, 4-cylinder

Engine power: 150 hp

Length: 2.8 metres

Weight: 250 kg

Snowmobiles ▽

In parts of North America, Scandinavia, Russia, and the polar regions, the ground is permanently covered with snow. ORVs can cope with thin or hard-packed snow, but a different type of vehicle is needed to go into the deep, off-road snow. Snowmobiles are small one- or two-person snow-bikes with skis and a **continuous track** instead of wheels. The engine drives the track. Steering is by means of turning the ski, or skis, at the front.

Off-road sport

Almost all types of motor vehicles, from lawn mowers to trucks, take part in motor racing. Off-road vehicles are raced against each other, too. They compete in some of the most extreme motorsport events in the world.

There are two main types of off-road racing that use two very different types of vehicles. Vehicles that look like ordinary production ORVs take part in races and rallies across deserts in the USA, Australia, Africa, the Middle East, and Asia. Some of them are, indeed, ordinary ORVs. Others are production models that have been specially prepared for racing. Formula Off Road racing is completely different. Its vehicles start out as standard off-roaders, but they are completely rebuilt, often with parts from other vehicles. They look like a collection of scrapyard leftovers bolted together, but they are extremely powerful and strong machines.

On safari ▽

The Australian Safari is one of the toughest tests of off-road vehicles and their drivers, and is over 5,000 kilometres long. The vehicles are modified as much as the regulations allow.

- Some of them are almost standard ORVs straight out of the showroom, with a few minor modifications for safety and long-range driving.
- Others are specially built for racing, with tougher **suspension**, a stronger under-body, and a race-tuned engine.

AN INTRODUCTORY GUIDE TO

Aromatherapy

Louise Tucker

General Editor Jane Foulston

Published by EMS Publishing
2nd Floor Chiswick Gate,
598-608 Chiswick High Road, London, W4 5RT
0845 017 9022

© Education and Media Services Ltd.

First published November 2000.
Revised July 2009.

ISBN 978 1903348147

Set in 10/13 Legacy.

Printed by hsw print

Prepared for the publishers by Idego Media Limited.

Acknowledgements

The publishers would like to thank the following for their invaluable assistance in the
preparation of this book:

Louise Barnes ITEC Qualified Aromatherapist and Beauty Therapist
Louise Oakley Model
Claire Bowman Photography
Isabella Panattoni Photography
Cariad and PA Aroma suppliers of essential oils for the photography
Rachael Kammerling Model
Briony Ruth Frayne Model

We would also like to acknowledge the assistance of the following
photographic agencies for supplying many of the images used:
Heather Angel
A-Z Botanical Collection Ltd
Harry Smith Horticultural Photographic Collection
Garden Matters
John Fielding Slide Library

AROMATHERAPY

Contents

Introduction

This book provides a clearly explained and illustrated introduction to aromatherapy. Ideal for students and professionals, it covers everything from the history of essential oils to their present-day uses and applications.

Author

Louise Tucker

Louise Tucker is a freelance writer. Previously an academic and tutor, she has written books on various subjects, including *An Introductory Guide to Anatomy and Physiology*, also published by Holistic Therapy Books.

General Editor

Jane Foulston

Jane Foulston has had a long career as a lecturer in anatomy and physiology for beauty and complementary therapy in private and FE colleges as well as setting up a school in Japan. She also has 15 years' experience as an external examiner for professional vocational qualifications. She lectured at East Berkshire College and Bridgewater College and her students have become practitioners in beauty therapy, aromatherapy and in a variety of sports therapies. She is currently Director of the International Therapy Examination Council.

Contributing Editors

Elaine Hall

Elaine Hall began her career teaching beauty and complementary therapies at the West of England College in Bath. She then went on to manage the complementary therapies section at Bridgwater College. Since then Elaine has run her own private salon and clinic based within a nursing home where she has treated both the elderly and private clients. In addition she has held the post of Senior ITEC Examiner and she examines extensively both in the South West of England and overseas, and is part of the qualifications development team.

Fae Major

Fae Major has worked in the beauty therapy industry for 23 years. She qualified with international diplomas in 1981, and her work has included three years working for Steiners International Hair and Beauty, one year in an alternative medicine clinic, two years in a small private salon in the north of England and a short spell in a salon in Barbados. For the last 16 years she has been teaching beauty therapy and aromatherapy, and in 1992 she became a practical examiner for ITEC, and has been a theory examination marker since 2002.

Marguerite Wynne

Marguerite Wynne began her career in one of London's foremost beauty salons and went on to teach in The College of Beauty Therapy in the West End. Subsequently, she owned her own clinic and school in Buckinghamshire, specialising in Complementary Therapies. She has been a Chief Examiner for ITEC since 1985 during which time she has spent three years based in the Far East.

DON'T FORGET TO
USE YOUR RESOURCE
CD ROM

- TEST YOUR KNOWLEDGE OF ESSENTIAL OILS

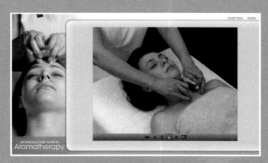

- TEST YOUR KNOWLEDGE QUESTIONS

- FULL VIDEO OF PRACTICAL SKILLS

AND MUCH MORE!

An introductory guide to Aromatherapy

1 The history and origins of aromatherapy

In Brief

Aromatherapy is the use of essential oils from plants for their therapeutic properties. The oils are used for treating medical and non-medical conditions. Although it may appear to be a relatively new therapy, plant oils have been used for their health benefits for centuries.

Learning objectives

The target knowledge of this chapter is:
- the history of aromatherapy
- the development of aromatherapy
- the definition of aromatherapy.

HISTORY

What is aromatherapy?

Aromatherapy is the systematic use of essential oils in holistic treatments to improve physical and emotional well-being. Essential oils, extracted from plants, possess distinctive therapeutic properties which can be used to improve health and prevent disease. Both their physiological and psychological effects combine well to promote positive health. These natural plant oils are applied in a variety of ways including massage, baths and inhalations. They are readily absorbed into the skin and have gentle physiological effects. Aromatherapy is an especially effective treatment for stress-related problems and a variety of chronic conditions. The name dates from the 1920s but different cultures and civilisations, such as the Ancient Egyptians and the Roman Empire, have used plants and herbs for religious, medical and cosmetic purposes, as well as in rituals, embalming and preserving, for centuries.

'The Cradle of Medicine'

The Egyptians are known to have used plant resins and essences in preserving the dead. Cedar and myrrh were used in embalming and jars of frankincense and styrax have been found by archaeologists in tombs dating from 3000BC. The antiseptic and antibacterial qualities of the oils and essences helped to prevent dead bodies from rotting so that, when mummies were discovered thousands of years later, they were perfectly preserved. In a hot country with little sanitation, plant extracts and oils made life more pleasant! Some of the prescriptions and formulae were inscribed onto stone tablets which is one of the reasons we know so much about them today.

The Greeks

The Nile Valley in Egypt was known as the 'Cradle of Medicine' and other cultures, especially the ancient Greeks gained much of their knowledge from travelling to this area and taking the information home. Hippocrates (born around 460BC) was a Greek and he was an important person in the development of the use of plants in medicine. He also wrote on the subject, thus helping others to understand the useful properties of plants and herbs.

The Arab influence

Any history of aromatherapy should mention a Persian called Abd Allah ibn Sina (980–1037), usually referred to as Avicenna, who contributed a great deal to medicine both past and present. Firstly, he described accurately about

An Egyptian sarcophagus

You can visit the remains of Roman baths in Bath, England.

eight hundred plants and their uses. Secondly, he devised very detailed instructions on massage and thirdly, he is credited with discovering the process of distillation by which most of our essential oils are obtained.

The first scented baths?

The Romans had a huge Empire, which existed for over 500 years (from 27BC until around the fifth century AD). They had conquered many other countries and had access to all the plants and oils of those countries. Oils and essences were an important part of Roman culture. For example, they were used at the public baths, in the water and in massage. This might not seem very significant to us, but baths were a central part of a Roman's daily life. They were like present-day cafés and pubs: this was where you went not only to get a wash and massage but also to chat to friends, family and business associates.

Four millennia of experience

China and India both have a long history of using plants and herbs and their extracts for medical purposes. In India medicine is aimed at healing the whole body i.e. treating physical, spiritual and psychological problems all at the same time. Traditional Indian herbal medicine, known as Ayurvedic medicine, dates from thousands of years ago as does Chinese medicine. Now, in 2000AD, 4000 years later, the use of Chinese medical treatments such as acupuncture, shiatsu or herbal remedies is becoming widespread.

From the Crusades to the Great Plague: Europe's role

Europe learnt about the health benefits of plants and herbs through the travels of knights and soldiers who brought back news of their use, especially after the Crusades (from the eleventh to the thirteenth century). Gradually,

THE HISTORY AND ORIGINS OF AROMATHERAPY

Europeans began to experiment with herbal remedies made from plants and herbs that grew in their own countries, like sage, lavender and rosemary. In the Middle Ages people protected themselves against infection by carrying plants, wearing herbal bouquets and throwing both over the floor. Through the ages, all classes of society used herbal medicines. A great advocate was Henry VIII, who in 1543 established a charter protecting the rights of herbalists to practice. By the 17th century the knowledge of herbal medicine was becoming widespread with publications such as 'The English Physician' by Nicholas Culpeper and 'The Great Herbal' by John Gerard documenting plants and their uses. During the Great Plague perfumers and apothecaries were thought to be immune from the disease. Using flowers and plants against germs might sound superstitious but think of how many lavender, pine and sandalwood disinfectants and cleaning products we now have in our lives! And gipsies still sell lucky bunches of herbs to ward off evil. Other natural healing systems were developed during the 18th and early 19th centuries from traditional backgrounds such as the water or nature cure. Naturopathy, a therapy based upon the use of diet, exercise, herbalism and hydrotherapy to prevent ill health was one such therapy which is still practised today.

Blinding with science

The development of chemistry and printing in the nineteenth century helped herbal and plant medicine in two ways. New chemical processes made it easier to extract oils and the invention of printing meant that lots of books on the

In the Bible, the three kings brought gifts to baby Jesus, including frankincense and myrrh.

● Did you know?

Frankincense means pure incense, from the Old French 'franc encens'. Though we might think that frankincense and myrrh are poor gifts compared to gold, we are using modern values to compare them. The fact that they were presented at an important event such as the birth of Jesus suggests that they were worth just as much if not more than gold. Frankincense is still used as part of the incense burned in some churches. See Adrian Room (Ed), *Brewer's Dictionary of Phrase and Fable*, p. 420.

subject, called herbals, were published. However, science helped both to develop the use of plants and herbs in medicines and to destroy it. It became easier and cheaper to discover some of the elements of plant oils, and their qualities, and attempt to produce synthetic versions of them. So commercial, mass-produced products and remedies using artificial ingredients replaced the natural formulas created for the individual person and problem. Allopathy was a term coined by homeopath Samuel Hahnnemann, to describe the new way of treating disease with medicines that produced effects different to those caused by the disease itself. Allopathic or conventional medicine gained popularity, with the new manufactured drugs seen as more effective than old remedies; conventional, scientific based medicine became the norm. Herbal medicine, using ancient and tested traditions was no longer taken seriously and was even considered 'quackery' compared to 'real' scientific medicine.

The 'invention' of aromatherapy

The term aromatherapy was coined by a French chemist called René Maurice Gattefossé in the 1920s. He was a chemist and perfumier who worked in his family perfumery business. One day he burnt his hand and plunged it into a vat of lavender oil to cool it down. He discovered that the lavender oil helped his burns to heal and prevented scarring. During the First World War (1914-1918) he used oils on soldiers' wounds and discovered that they helped heal wounds much faster. He went on to research the therapeutic properties of essential oils and first used the phrase *aromathérapie* in a scientific research paper he delivered in 1928. Several other French scientists, including Dr Jean Valnet, continued the research into the effect of essential oils on physical burns and wounds as well as psychological disorders. Valnet also used oils on soldiers' wounds, through his work as an army doctor during the war in Indo-China (1948-59), using their antiseptic qualities and abilities to

Did you know?

In China, the Yellow Emperor's Book of Internal Medicine is one of the earliest records of the use of herbal medicine, dating back to at least 2000 years BC. See Julia Lawless, *The Encyclopaedia of Essential Oils*, p. 12.

THE HISTORY AND ORIGINS OF AROMATHERAPY

A field of lavender

combat disease to great effect. Valnet also advocated taking essential oils internally and the management of health through a natural diet.

Aromatherapy reaches Britain

Marguerite Maury, an Austrian biochemist and follower of the work of Valnet, is the person responsible for bringing aromatherapy to Britain. She had discovered that when she used essential oils in massage the skin absorbed the oils very well. In the 1940s she brought her ideas for massage treatments using essential oils to this country and, with the help of several people (including Micheline Arcier, Dr W. E. Arnould-Taylor, Eve Taylor and Dr Jean Valnet) she set up aromatherapy practices. Her students then set up their own practices and the interest in this method of treatment has been growing ever since. Further more, although first established as a beauty therapy treatment, aromatherapy was developed as a clinical (i.e. medical) therapy by Robert Tisserand who published 'The Art of Aromatherapy' in 1977.

Full circle

Thanks to Gattefossé and his followers, aromatherapy began to be taken seriously again. The reputation of complementary therapies is now coming full circle. A move away from orthodox medicine and commercial drugs has coincided with, or perhaps caused a surge of interest in the use of natural complementary therapies. Traditional medicine is now beginning to recognise the value of complementary therapies. Aromatherapy is now offered alongside orthodox practices in many healthcare settings worldwide. The establishment of voluntary regulatory bodies and formal training programmes have raised the standards within the industry and increased public and professional awareness of the therapy. A healthy lifestyle is now recognised as a means to prevent ill health and is actively encouraged. Aromatherapy continues to play an important part in the holistic management of health and wellbeing.

Research

As aromatherapy becomes increasingly popular, the demands to prove the claims for its efficacy become more pressing. Scientific research is seen as validation of a therapy, meeting and protecting the needs of interested parties. However, there are many difficulties encountered when undertaking clinical research procedures to test complementary therapy and its applications. The human factor, placebo effect and natural variations in the quality of oils may all affect aromatherapy test results. Aromatherapists need to be aware of developments and analysis within their field and the results, both positive and negative. Ongoing research is essential and has important implications for the legislation and regulation of the industry.

2 Essential oils and where they come from

In Brief

In order to understand the present-day use of plant and herb oils in aromatherapy and other treatments, we need to learn exactly what an essential oil is. The following section provides a definition and description of essential oils as well as explaining the different methods for extracting them from plants.

WHAT ARE ESSENTIAL OILS?

Useful Tip
Crush a leaf or the petal of a an aromatic plant between your fingers: your fingers will be scented with the plant's essential oil.

Essential oils are aromatic, volatile substances extracted from a single botanical source by distillation or expression. They are found in leaves, flowers, seeds, plant stems, twigs, tree bark, resin, heartwood roots, fruit pulp and peel. Similar to animal hormones, they are sometimes referred to as the plants' 'life force'. Generally, the cells containing them are close to the surface but they can only be seen with the help of a microscope, not just by looking at a leaf or flower. The essence is either stored in the cell where it is made or, as is the case with citrus fruits, moved to special storage sacs.

Essential oils or essences as they are also known are:

- aromatic – have a distinctive and often fragrant smell
- volatile – evaporate quickly in the air and to varying degrees depending on the oil
- very powerful when neat – are usually blended with a carrier oil for massage purposes (see Chapter 4)
- flammable – must be kept in a cool place away from heat and/or naked flames
- soluble in oil (lipophilic) and alcohol (in water they will form a suspension i.e. particles of the oil can be suspended in the water but will not mix with it being only slightly hydrophilic)
- liquid – exceptions include rose otto and benzoin which are semi-solid
- non-greasy – despite their name, the oils are generally light and not oily!
- expensive – producing the plants and extracting the oil is labour intensive and thus costly.

You now know what an essential oil is. The next section explains how they are extracted: how they get from the plant to the bottle!

WHERE DO THEY COME FROM?

A NOTE ON PRICE

The price of an oil reflects two main factors: the time and energy required to produce and harvest the plants and the weight of material or number of flowers required to produce a certain amount of oil. Since there is more oil contained in a leaf than in a petal, oils from leaves will be cheaper than oils from flowers. So sage, thyme and rosemary, from leaves, will be cheaper than jasmine or rose which come from petals. This means that the amount of raw material required to produce different oils varies enormously: whereas only 400kg of thyme will produce 1kg of essential thyme oil, 2000kg of rose petals are needed to produce 1kg of rose oil. And to obtain just 1kg of jasmine oil, one of the most expensive available, four million jasmine flowers are needed...and, since they can only be harvested by hand, in the afternoon and evening, the production process is very expensive!

Essential oils come from various parts of the plants. Some plants only produce one oil e.g.

- basil oil – from basil leaves
- fennel – from fennel seeds
- pine – from the needles and sometimes the cones of pine trees.

Other plants produce several oils from different parts. For example, the orange tree can produce three essential oils:

- petitgrain – from the leaves and twigs
- neroli – from the blossom
- orange – from the peel of the fruit.

EXTRACTION METHODS

How do the oils get from the plant to the bottle?

The first stage of production is growing the plants! This process, like every other process in the essential oil industry is labour intensive and therefore expensive. This is because the plants must be looked after very carefully, sometimes by hand (to prevent machinery causing damage and wasting the oil). Once harvested, the plants need to be processed in order to extract the essential oils. There are seven methods of extraction:

- steam or water distillation
- expression
- solvent extraction
- carbon dioxide extraction
- hydro-diffusion/percolation
- enfleurage
- maceration (an old method which is rarely used today).

Steam distillation/ Water distillation

This is the most common and economical method of extraction. Plant material is placed in the first part of a still (see diagram). It is either mixed with water which is then heated to produce steam or steam under pressure is passed through the plant material. The heat from the water or steam causes the essential oil in the plant material to break down and evaporate. The mix of steam and oil vapour passes into a cooled pipe and condenses (turns back into liquid). The now-liquid mix passes into a collecting vessel where the oil and water, which are of different densities, separate making it easy to decant the oil. There are five stages to distillation:

1. **plant preparation**: flowers and leaves and any non-woody or fibrous parts of plants can be put in the still as they are. But if the oil is from a wood (like sandalwood or rosewood) or a seed (like carrot seed) then the raw material needs to be prepared. Woody parts, like branches or twigs must be grated; anything with a husk or shell (seeds) must be crushed and fruits must be cut. This is necessary to break the walls of the plants' oil cells and release the oil.

2. **heat**: in steam distillation the raw material (leaves, petals, wood etc) has steam from a separate tank passed through it under pressure. This method is particularly suited to plant material that deteriorates rapidly after harvest, for example flowers. Distillation times are dependent on the nature of the plant material; in water distillation the raw material is placed directly into the water which is then brought to boiling point.

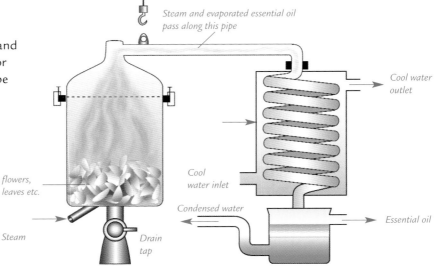

Distillation plant.

Steam and evaporated essential oil pass along this pipe

Cool water outlet

flowers, leaves etc.

Cool water inlet

Condensed water

Steam

Drain tap

Essential oil

ESSENTIAL OILS AND WHERE THEY COME FROM

3. **evaporation**: the heat makes the oil cells release their essence and the oil evaporates into the steam.

4. **condensation**: the steam and the vapour it contains collect in a pipe and are transported to a condenser (a coiled pipe which is immersed in a tank of cold water). As soon as the hot steam and vapour come into contact with the cold pipe, they begin to condense i.e. they turn back into liquids.

5. **collection**: the steam condenses and becomes very lightly scented water, (known as aromatic waters or hydrolats) whereas the plant's oil, which is not the same density as water floats to the top of the 'liquefied steam' or sinks to the bottom (depending on the oil). The essential oil can now be collected.

A solvent extractor.

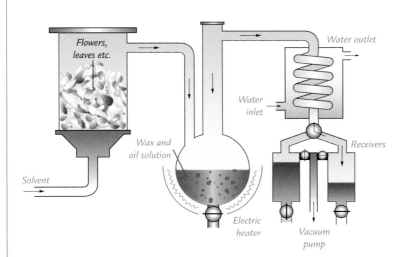

NB The heat used in steam distillation may alter some of the essential oil molecules. Thus the evacuated steam distillation method is sometimes used commercially to avoid this problem. This involves taking as much air as possible out of the distilling equipment (hence 'evacuated') which reduces the air pressure inside. The water used to create the steam therefore boils at a lower temperature which lessens the damage to the oil.

Hydro-diffusion/Percolation

Percolation uses steam in a similar way to distillation but it percolates down though the plant material instead of up. When cooled at the bottom of the tank the oil either floats or sinks, depending on the density and is easily separated. Percolation's main advantage is that it is faster than distillation, which results in less damage to the oil because the essence is heated for a shorter period of time.

Expression

The oils of citrus fruits (e.g. orange, lemon, grapefruit, mandarin and bergamot) are contained in tiny sacs in the peel. These oils are extracted by the application of pressure. The fruit's pulp and pith are removed and the peel is squeezed to release its oil. Expression used to be done by hand (the oil was collected on sponges) but now, due to the enormous demand for essential oils, machines are used.

NB Strictly speaking, expression extracts the plant's pure essence rather than its essential oil, since the oil obtained is exactly the same as that contained in the plant whereas essential oils are not exactly the same composition as the essence because they have come into contact with other substances, like water or solvents, or been heated. Any oil extracted by a cold, pressed method (i.e. one that simply uses pressure and no heat) is a true essence. This is a bit like olive oil: extra virgin olive oil, i.e. the best and purest, is cold-pressed because the olives have simply been crushed, no heat has been used and no change in composition has taken place.

Solvent extraction

Solvent extraction is the method used when the aromatic essence is difficult to obtain by distillation (e.g. resinoids) or when the process of distillation might damage the delicate fragrance of the plant (e.g. rose and jasmine). There are three types:

● **resinoid e.g. benzoin, myrrh**
When the bark of a tree or a bush is cut it seems to bleed: a liquid escapes from the cut which solidifies when it comes into contact with air. This semi-solid substance is known as a resin or gum. The aromatic essence of these resins is difficult to obtain through distillation because they are often mixed up with tough fibrous material such as bark and dirt. There are three stages for extracting a resinoid:

1. *preparation*: the raw material is chopped and cut, then placed on a rack in a clean vessel and covered with solvents such as hydrocarbons (e.g. benzene or hexane) or alcohols.

2. *heat*: the mixture is gently heated and the oils contained in the woody plant material dissolve in the solvent.

3. *filtration*: the solvent is evaporated off and the solid residue is called a resinoid.

● **concrete**
When a plant's essential oil is damaged by the hot water or steam used in distillation (for example the fragrance of jasmine flowers is affected by water), solvent extraction is used instead to obtain a solid substance called a concrete, a mixture of natural waxes and a plant's aromatic essence. They are highly concentrated and more 'stable' (i.e they do not evaporate when exposed to the air) than pure

essential oils. Similar to resin extraction, this process uses hydrocarbon solvents and has three stages:

1. *preparation*: the raw material is put on racks in clean sealed vessels and covered with solvent.

2. *heat*: the mixture is gently heated and the solvent dissolves the essences contained in the plant material.

3. *filtration*: the liquid that remains is filtered to remove the solvent. The semi-solid paste that remains is the concrete.

● **absolutes e.g. rose, jasmine**
After extraction concretes are usually treated further to obtain what is known as an absolute. Absolutes are obtained by mixing a concrete (or a pomade from enfleurage – see below) with alcohol. The aromatic plant essence transfers from the solid waxy substance to the alcohol and the wax which is not soluble in alcohol is left as residue. This process has two stages:

1. *mixing*: the concrete is mixed with alcohol and then chilled. The plant essence in the concrete dissolves in the alcohol and a waxy residue remains.

2. *filtration*: the solution is filtered to separate the waxy residue from the liquid. Then the alcohol is evaporated off, leaving the absolute, the plant's essence.

What is an absolute?

A liquid which is thicker and more highly concentrated than a pure essential oil. Some are solids or semi-solid such as rose absolute, which may solidify at room temperature but turns into a liquid when it gets warmer. Absolutes are generally used in small amounts not only

Enfleurage trays

because they are so highly concentrated but also because they may still contain a residue of the extraction solvent and this can cause reactions.

Enfleurage

This is an old extraction process that produces a waxy substance, similar to a concrete, known as a pomade. It is very labour-intensive and therefore expensive and is rarely used except when the very highest quality oil is required. It only works with flowers which carry on producing essential oils after they have been harvested. The process involves four stages:

1. **extraction**: flowers and petals are placed on trays which have been coated with animal fat. They are left on the trays for several days and the fat absorbs the plant essence. Faded petals are replaced with fresh ones until the fat is completely saturated with the essence.

2. **collection**: the fat is removed from the trays and any remaining petals taken out. The 'aromatic fat' is now known as a pomade.

3. **separation**: the pomade is mixed in alcohol and agitated constantly for a day (this part is carried out by a machine) so that the essential oil can separate from the fat. The fat is removed.

4. **evaporation**: the alcohol is evaporated off from the mixture leaving the enfleurage absolute.

Like other absolutes, those from enfleurage are highly concentrated and are either thick liquids or solids.

Maceration

Maceration is a process similar to enfleurage by which plant material is placed in liquid fixed oils or fat and then heated to 60–70°C. The mixture is stirred and the heat causes the cells containing essential oils to break down, allowing the constituents to be absorbed by the oil or fat. The plant material is then removed and the process repeated until the fixed oil or fat is saturated. The strained plant material is wrapped in bags and cold pressed to obtain any remaining liquid. If fat is used it is called a pomade and can be treated with alcohol as above to produce an absolute.

Infusion

This is a simple method of essential oil extraction that can be used at home with herbs from the garden to make pleasantly scented massage oil. Plant material is placed in a fixed oil and left in a warm place. The essential oils are gradually absorbed by the fixed oils and the plant material is separated. This process can be repeated until the desired concentration is achieved. Calendula is an example of an infused oil.

Carbon dioxide extraction

This is quite a new process that dates from the 1980s. It is similar to solvent extraction, in that plant material is brought into contact with a chemical substance, in this case, compressed carbon dioxide (CO_2) at a low temperature. The process is quite complicated and therefore expensive.

You now know where essential oils come from and how they are extracted. The final section in this chapter explains the factors that affect oil quality, some of the different uses of oils and the benefits of using good quality oils.

THE QUALITY OF ESSENTIAL OILS

The previous section explained how essential oils and essences are extracted from all sorts of plants. Production and extraction, as you can see, are time-consuming, laborious and costly which makes the oils very expensive. This, combined with increased demand for essential oils, has created a market for cheaper, poorer quality, artificial or synthetic oils and diluted versions. The next section explains how and why companies and individuals 'adulterate' oils and why oil quality is so important in aromatherapy.

What is adulteration?

Both companies and individuals may adulterate (i.e. change) an expensive pure oil to make it go further and, in some cases make more money. Essential oils can be adulterated in several ways:

1. **dilution**: the essential oil is diluted with fixed oils, chemicals such as Diacetone alcohol or Poyethelene glycols, cheaper oils and synthetic oils. All of these results in a finished product of inferior quality with differing therapeutic properties from the authentic essence it purports to be.

2. **isolation**: a chemical from a cheaper oil may be isolated, removed and mixed with the expensive oil to make it go further e.g. a chemical from lemongrass, which is relatively cheap, is mixed with the very expensive melissa oil.

3. **substitution**: a cheaper oil may be used instead e.g. amyris may be substituted for sandalwood.

It is difficult not only to know the contents of these diluted and adulterated blends but also to detect the synthetic versions. A qualified aromatherapist will always use a reputable supplier, especially since an adulterated oil may not work effectively in treatment.

Why is it important to use real, unadulterated oils?

Artificial and synthetic oils and the diluted versions do not have the same therapeutic effects. It is the plant's essence, not a copy of its essence or a tenth of its essence mixed with another oil, which has healing qualities. Egyptian mummies are unlikely to have been so well-preserved if they had been embalmed with adulterated plant essences! The pure oil is made up of hundreds of different chemical constituents, many of which are still unknown to scientists, and mixed together they produce a particular synergy, and this synergistic force and blend cannot be copied by a synthetic substance. It is important to be able to identify the correct oil or essence. Buy only from reputable suppliers. Wholesalers will identify the country of origin, botanical and common name, provide batch and bottling identification numbers, methods of use, contraindications and indications for use, and use by dates. If in any doubt about the source or quality of an oil, do not buy it!

Methods of testing oil quality

Suppliers have many ways of testing the quality of an essential oil purchased from producers and importers. Essences undergo several forms of testing to identify their chemical constituents and quality.

Organoleptic/Sensory testing

Suppliers will initially evaluate an oil by sensory means. Usually performed by a professional 'nose', the viscosity of an oil, colour and odour will all be checked.

These tests, however, are subjective but enable an initial assessment of an essence prior to further analysis.

Gas chromatography

The essence is vaporised and the chemical constituents evaporate at differing rates. A flame ionisation detector registers this evaporation as a series of peaks and troughs on a chart – a chromatograph. This is the oil's 'fingerprint'. The peaks and troughs chart the quantities of chemical constituents found in an essence. Readings are compared to standard charts to identify authenticity.

Infra-red spectrophotometry

This measures the rates at which molecules vibrate in the presence of Infra Red light. This test is used to identify the chemical constituents of an essence. Readings are then compared to industry standards.

Optical rotation/Refractive Index

These tests use light waves to check the quality of an oil; industry standards are then used to clarify readings.

Other tests, which may be performed, include Specific Gravity, Ph testing, and Mass Spectrometry. Professional suppliers of essences and fixed oils must be able to provide information on chemical analysis of their products to customers.

Degradation/Spoilage

From plant, through production to end product, an essential oil or essence may degrade and lose its potency if handled incorrectly. Extended storage periods or incorrect storage in light, heat and air will cause the oil to chemically break down and alter the therapeutic effects through processes such as oxidation or hydrolysis. These chemical changes may also make the oil hazardous. Essences and fixed oils have a shelf life and the manufacturer or supplier should record the expiry date on the bottle. Cold pressed citrus oils are the quickest to degrade. Most oils are thought to have a shelf life of approximately 2 years, although some oils such as rose absolute are thought to improve with age and last up to 5 years.

What is synergy?

The word synergy comes from Greek: the syn comes from the Greek sun, meaning with or together; ergy comes from the greek ergon to work i.e. to work together. Synergy or a synergistic effect in aromatherapy means that when two or more oils work together they produce more of an effect than they do alone. Research has been done on the individual chemical constituents of essential oils and their qualities and effects; what isn't known is how they work together and/or produce effects that are not expected given their chemical make-up and what is known about them.

Can anyone benefit from using synthetics?

Yes, industry. The perfume, pharmaceutical and food industries use essential oils to give their products pleasant smells and flavours e.g. peppermint is used in toothpaste and chewing gum. They need standard smells, not those that are subject to environmental change caused by temperature, storage conditions and where the plant was cultivated. For their purposes synthetic fragrances are preferable because they can produce the same aroma, and thus the same product, over and over again. It does not matter to the food industry that the therapeutic effects of a particular oil are no longer effective!

Other factors affecting the quality of oils

Like good wines, good oils have a vintage and a vineyard! Plants and essential oils, just like grapes and the wine they eventually produce, are affected by where, when and how they are grown. They are influenced by similar factors: the soil quality, rainfall, temperature, the climate, altitude, the location where the plants are grown, the source of the plant, the quality of the cultivation process, methods of harvesting, when the plant is harvested and how it is looked after once it is harvested, the part of the plant used to produce the oil, the method of extraction, the storage conditions of the finished essence/oil, and any adulteration.

DON'T FORGET TO USE YOUR RESOURCE CD ROM

- TEST YOUR KNOWLEDGE OF ESSENTIAL OILS

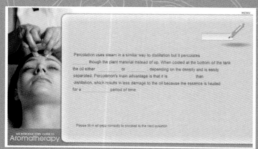

- TEST YOUR KNOWLEDGE QUESTIONS

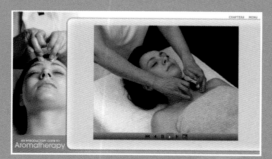

- FULL VIDEO OF PRACTICAL SKILLS

AND MUCH MORE!

An introductory guide to Aromatherapy

3 Botany

The target knowledge of this chapter is:
- the definition of taxonomy and nomenclature
- why plant families are important to the aromatherapist
- Understanding of the basic structure of plants

In Brief

It is useful for the aromatherapist to have an understanding of basic botany, plant names and the plant families. This information is important when selecting essences and fixed oils for treatment. Plant names ensure that the aromatherapist selects the correct oils for their properties, avoiding those that are sub-standard or not suitable for therapy.

BOTANY

Taxonomy – the science that finds describes, classifies, identifies and names organisms – in this instance, plants.

Nomenclature – the application or assignment of names.

Plant classification

Throughout history millions of plants have been discovered and documented as both food and medicines. Some plant names developed from the plant use or the area in which they grew. Latin was the common language used by the medical and scientific world to describe them and plants were often given long Latin names. This science is called taxonomy.

Carl Linnaeus (1707-1778) was a Swedish naturalist who refined the basic Latin system into a standardized system for plants and animals. He reduced the complex names into a 2 part or binomial system: firstly- the generic name (genus), secondly- the specific name (species). He produced comprehensive documentation for both botanists and zoologists in the mid 1700's, which quickly became widely accepted and adopted. This system is still in use today – for example Melaleuca. The second name applies to one specific plant only and often describes the plant. The generic name has a capital letter and the specific name does not, for example Melaleuca viridiflora. So Niaouli belongs to the genus Melaleuca and the species Melaleuca viridiflora. Tea tree – Melaleuca alternifolia belongs to the same genus. A third name often denotes a chemotype.

Chemotypes

What are chemotypes?

Chemotypes are botanically identical plants that produce chemically different oils. So two lavender plants may look exactly the same but the chemical composition of their oils will vary. This is caused by the factors mentioned previously, for example: where and when they are grown, the climate, soil quality for extraction, time of harvest and techniques used (e.g. by hand or machine), the altitude plants are grown at and the quality of the cultivation. If this difference in chemical make-up alters the oil's properties and effects, this is known as a chemotype and the oil may be labelled as such. It is worth remembering that chemotypes are not unnatural and have not been adulterated in any way: they are just chemically different because they have consistently been grown in a particular place or for a specific reason. So, for example, essential oil specialists may sell lavender plus a chemotype lavender, one may be grown at a high altitude and the other at sea level: the difference in altitude affects the chemical composition. Such plants may also be given a third name – a trinomial. These are usually to describe the chemotype, for example Thymus vulgaris ct. linalool or Thymus vulgaris ct. thymol. The third name here describes the specific chemical composition of a particular chemotype.

Useful Tip

To try and remember what a chemotype is think about wine! Wine comes from grapevines and depending on where the vines are grown the grapes and the wine they produce will be completely different. An Australian white wine that uses the same grape variety, like chardonnay, as a French white wine will taste very different: in some senses they are chemotypes.

PLANT IDENTIFICATION

A plant family is a group of plants with a similar structure.

The plant kingdom is split into divisions or phyla. The division we are concerned with is the Spermatophyta – or the plants that produce seeds. This splits into a subphylum containing Gymnosperm (seeds borne in the open on cones e.g conifer) and Angiosperm (flowering plants that produce covered seeds)

In addition to the Conifers, essences are only found in plants belonging to the Angiosperm subphylum, which is broken down further into two classes – Monocotyledons and Dicotyledons.

Monocotyledons are plants with a single leaf, narrow, non-woody parallel leaves and small flowers for wind pollination – for example grass, vetiver, lemongrass.

Dicotyledons are plants with two seed leaves; they can be woody or non-woody with broad net-veined leaves and floral parts in multiples of four or five – for example Sweet Marjoram, Geranium.

Within a species a variety or a cultivar may exist. A variety originates naturally as a result of mutations. The mutation still closely resembles the originals and

can be interbred with them to form fertile offspring. A cultivar is a plant that has undergone cultivation i.e. been grown for a specific purpose or properties. These are often given the name of the grower.

Useful Tip

To remember cultivar think
CULTIvated **VAR**iety.

PLANT STRUCTURE

Root

Most roots hold the plant in the ground and may be branching or tap like, for example carrot. Microscopic root hairs take in the water and nutrients that a plant needs for growth.

Rhizome

A modified stem growing just below the surface of the soil in a horizontal direction e.g. ginger.

Stem

Stems provide support for the plant, permit the transportation of water and nutrients and support the leaves, flowers and fruit. Some long lived plants develop thick stems that turn woody with age.

Leaf

Leaves are the energy converter, they absorb sunlight and using chlorophyll, a green pigment, transform carbon dioxide from air and water into carbohydrates used for growth. This process, known as photosynthesis, produces oxygen.

Flowers

Plants reproduce themselves using flowers, attracting pollinating insects so that pollen from the stamen, or male part, of one flower is transferred to the carpel, or female part of the same or another flower. Pollen from the anther needs to reach the stigma for fertilisation. The female part of the flower once fertilised can then produce a fruit containing seeds to continue plant propagation. Single flowers can be held on a stalk or occur in a group on a stalk – this is known as infloresence.

Fruit

Some plants produce fruit to hold their seeds (Angiosperms). These may be eaten by animals, birds or dispersed by the wind.

Seeds

Plants have evolved to spread their seeds and continue new plant life. Plant seeds are surrounded by seed coat-Testa. They contain the plant embryo, the cotyledon and one or two proto leaves that will become the seedling when the right conditions are encountered.

Examples of the plant sources of essences and fixed oils can be found within chapters 5 and 6.

PLANT FAMILIES

- **Annonaceae**
  A mostly tropical family of plants consisting of trees and shrubs. This contains only one species – Cananga odorata; one of the two varieties is Ylang ylang

- **Apiaceae (Umbelliferae)**
  Aromatic plants with hollow stems. The plants have umbrella-like heads, hence the name. May be hazardous due to phenol or ketone content. Digestive oils – fennel.

- **Arecaceae**
  Palm family of flowering plants, palms are one of the most well-known and extensively cultivated plant families. Moisturising oil – e.g. coconut.

- **Asteraceae (Compositae)**
  These plants have daisy-like flowers. They have anti-inflammatory, calming properties – Chamomiles.

- **Burseraceae**
  A family often known as the 'incense family', containing trees and shrubs. Healing, expectorant properties – frankincense and myrrh.

- **Corylaceae**
  Known as the Birch Family, deciduous nut-bearing trees and shrubs about 130 species, which includes hazel. Slightly astringent, natural sun filter – e.g. hazelnut oil.

- **Cupressaceae**
  Part of the conifer family, trees and shrubs up to 116 m in height, the bark of mature trees is commonly orange- to red- brown and of stringy texture. Removes impurities and toxins – e.g. cypress and juniper.

- **Euphorbiaceae**
  Part of the family, is a large family of flowering plants. Most are herbs but some, especially in the tropics, are also shrubs or trees. Some are succulent and resemble cacti. Moisturising properties – e.g. castor oil.

- **Fabaceae (Leguminosae)**
  Is a large and economically important family of flowering plants, which is commonly known as the legume family, range from giant trees to small annual herbs. Emollient e.g. soya.

- **Geraniaceae**
Flowering plant family of over 800 species they are herbs or sub shrubs, most species are found in temperate or warm temperate regions, though some are tropical. Uplifting and stimulates circulation e.g. geranium.

- **Juglandaceae**
Also known as the Walnut Family, is a family of trees or sometimes shrubs. The trees are wind-pollinated, the flowers usually arranged in catkins, and the fruit is a true botanical nut. Emollient e.g walnut oil.

- **Lamiaceae (Labiatae)**
Also known as the mint family, it is the largest plant family of interest to the aromatherapist – with many properties, all parts of the plant are aromatic. Some are shrubs, but rarely trees or vines. Uplifts mind and body e.g. lavender and rosemary.

- **Lauraceae**
Or Laurel family comprises a group of flowering plants, over 2000 (perhaps as many as 4000) species world-wide, mostly from warm or tropical regions. Moisturises and protects skin e.g. avocado.

- **Linaceae**
Is a family of flowering plants, mostly herbaceous or rarely woody plants, sometimes large trees in the tropics. Emollient e.g. linseed oil.

- **Malvales**
Also sometimes identified as Steruliaceae. A group of flowering plants which contains the cacao tree (Theobroma cacao) used in the production of chocolate and cocoa butter.

- **Myrtaceae**
Or Myrtle family are a family. The oils from this plant family are highly volitile as the oil is stored in small pockets in the leaves. Has at least 3000 species, possibly more than 5000 species. Antiseptic and stimulant e.g. tea tree and eucalyptus.

- **Oleaceae**
Or olive family, is a plant family containing 600 species of shrubs, trees and occasionally vines. As shrubs, members of this family may be twine climbers, or scramblers. Emollient e.g. olive oil.

- **Onagraceae**
Also known as the Willowherb family or Evening Primrose family, is a family of flowering plants. The family includes about 640-650 species of herbs, shrubs, and trees. Anti-inflammatory e.g. evening primrose oil.

- **Pedaliaceae**
Pedalium family or sesame family is a flowering plant family, characterized by having mucilaginous hairs, which often give the stems and leaves a slimy or clammy feel, and often have fruits with hooks or horns. Emollient e.g. sesame oil.

- **Piperaceae**
Is the botanical name for a family of flowering plants, it is sometimes known as the "pepper family". The best known species is Piper nigrum, which yields the most famous peppercorns used as a spice, including "black pepper". Stimulant e.g. black pepper.

- **Pinaceae**
  Also known as the pine family includes many of the well-known conifers of commercial importance such as cedars, firs, hemlocks, larches, pines and spruces, with between 220-250 species. They are trees, rarely shrubs, growing from 2 to 100 m tall, mostly evergreen. Invigorating e.g. cedarwood.

- **Poaceae (Graminae)**
  Or Gramineae, plants of this family are usually called grasses, there are between 9,000–10,000 species of grasses. Plant communities dominated by Poaceae are called grasslands; it is estimated that grasslands comprise 20% of the vegetation cover of the earth. Refreshing e.g. lemongrass, vetivert.

- **Proteaceae**
  Is a family of flowering plants. Mainly restricted to the Southern Hemisphere, it is a fairly large family, with around 2000 species. Inhibit skin and cell ageing e.g. macadamia nut oil.

- **Rosaceae**
  Or rose family is a large family of plants, with about 3,000-4,000 species. Relaxing e.g. rose damask.

- **Rutaceae**
  Commonly known as the Rue or Citrus family. Species of the family generally have flowers that divide into four or five parts, usually with strong scents. They range in form and size from herbs to shrubs and small trees. Uplifting and have anti-depressant properties e.g. bergamot and petitgrain.

- **Santalaceae**
  Is a widely distributed family of flowering plants which, like other members of Santalales, are partially parasitic on other plants, approximately 1,000 species. Calming e.g. sandalwood.

- **Sapotaceae**
  Family of trees and shrubs, found in tropical regions – Shea or Karite tree that produces nut butter.

- **Simmondsiaceae**
  Or the Jojoba Family is a family of flowering plants. It consists of a single species only, jojoba (Simmondsia chinensis), of North American shrubs. Anti-inflammatory and moisturising e.g. jojoba oil.

- **Styracaceae**
  Is a small family of flowering plants with about 160 species of trees and shrubs, most are large shrubs to small trees 3-15 m tall. The family occurs in warm temperate and subtropical regions of the Northern Hemisphere. Warming e.g. benzoin.

- **Vitaceae**
  Are a family of flowering plants including the grape and Virginia creeper. The family name is derived from the genus Vitis which has about 60 species of vining plants. Protects and nourishes the skin e.g. grapeseed oil.

- **Zingiberaceae**
  Or the Ginger family, is a family of flowering plants consisting of aromatic perennial herbs with creeping horizontal or tuberous rhizomes, there are more than 1300 species, distributed throughout tropical Africa, Asia and the Americas. Stimulant e.g. ginger oil.

4 How aromatherapy works

Learning objectives ●

The target knowledge of this chapter is:
● the chemistry of essential oils
● why the chemistry is important
● how oils penetrate the body
● the structure and function of the olfactory tract
● the general effect of oils on the body
● the specific effect of oils on particular systems.

In Brief

The name aromatherapy might make you think that this treatment works solely through the aromas, i.e. the smell of plants. However, although the smell of a plant or herb is very important for the therapy to be effective (for example, if a patient doesn't like the smell of an oil the treatment is unlikely to work very well!) it is not the only factor to consider. Essential oils are very complex chemical structures and in order to understand their properties and effects (i.e. what they do and how to use them) it is helpful to know a little about their chemistry.

THE CHEMISTRY OF ESSENTIAL OILS

Humans have a very complicated chemical structure and so do the fluids that flow around their bodies. This is also true of plants; they are structurally and chemically complex and hold within essential oils, which some people refer to as the 'life force' of the plant. The following section explains a little about the chemistry of these oils.

How does a plant grow?

When we think of the growth of a living structure, whether a plant or a human, we think of it getting bigger and developing. What enables this change in size or structure are the chemicals. Everything around us, whether organic (living) or not (inorganic) is made up of chemicals continually changing and growth happens because the chemical structure of a living thing is developing.

For example, humans and plants are made of three main chemical elements: carbon, hydrogen and oxygen plus thousands of trace elements. Humans take these chemicals into their body, by breathing (air), drinking (water) and eating, and make proteins with them which are used for growth and repair. Plants absorb the chemical elements found in soil, in water and in air (carbon, hydrogen, oxygen, nitrogen and other elements) and use these to make proteins, for growth and repair,

carbohydrates and essential oils. The natural process of turning simple elements into complex chemical groups is known as *biosynthesis*.

So how does a plant make chemicals into leaves and flowers?

Every leaf and flower is made of millions of tiny fragments of chemical elements known as atoms. These atoms link up to make groups of atoms known as molecules which, in turn, join together to form all the different parts of a plant; the leaves, the flowers and the essential oil.

In plants, the link between a simple element – e.g. an atom of carbon or an atom of hydrogen on its own – and a complex group – e.g. a collection of atoms joined together, known as a *molecule* – is the energy of the sun. The sun's energy is captured by the plant's chlorophyll (the green pigment in the leaves) and used to convert the carbon dioxide in the air into other organic substances, in a process known as photosynthesis. Carbon and oxygen are the products of this: the carbon is used to make organic compounds (hydrocarbons and sugars) and some of the oxygen is released. The plant then uses this sugar to feed itself and grow. Plants also take the chemical elements in

C H O

The symbols are used to represent atoms of carbon, hydrogen and oxygen.

water and the soil, break them down into simple elements and then convert them into organic compounds it can use. This is called biosynthesis.

These basic metabolisms keep a plant alive. However, further metabolic changes occur in the plant, and one of the products of these is essential oil.

What is an atom?
An atom is the smallest possible unit of a chemical element. It is microscopic and attaches itself to other atoms in order to make bigger structures, known as molecules.

What is a molecule?
A molecule is a structure made of two or more atoms joined together. Molecules have particular qualities depending on how much of each chemical element they contain and the way in which those elements are arranged i.e. their shape. Each plant, and in particular each essential oil, has a different combination of molecules arranged in a different pattern. In a way a plant is a combination of different ingredients and it is this chemical 'recipe' and its arrangement which gives each essential oil its individual aroma, therapeutic qualities and effects.

Why are molecules of any interest to the aromatherapist?
Each molecule of an essential oil produces a particular effect and has a specific therapeutic quality. Thus, if an aromatherapist knows which oil, or which family of oils, contain which molecules, she/he will understand which oils to use for particular treatments. The main groups of molecules that are important to the aromatherapist, specifically because their effects and actions have been studied, are *terpenes*, *diterpenes*, *sesquiterpenes*, *esters*, *aldehydes*, *ketones*,

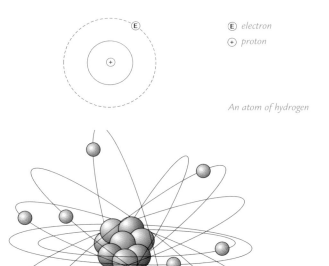

(E) *electron*
(+) *proton*

An atom of hydrogen

A molecule of oxygen

lactones, alcohols, phenols, oxides, acids, ethers and furanocoumarins. Terpene molecules, which are made of the atoms of hydrogen and carbon joined together, are known as hydrocarbons whereas all the other molecule groups contain oxygen as well as hydrogen and carbon and are known as oxygenated compounds. The following list gives the main properties and effects of each group.

Terpenes – end in 'ene'
A large number of hydrocarbons, found in most essential oils and formulated from the isoprene unit, which is made up of 5 carbon atoms in a branched chain. Monoterpenes are formed from 2 isoprene units/10 carbon atoms Sesquiterenes are formed from 3 isoprene units/ 15 carbon atoms Diterpenes are formed from 4 isoprene units/20 carbon atoms

Monoterpenes – end in 'ene' and may have Greek letter prefix
Effects are bactericidal, antiseptic,

Did you know?
Water is a molecule which links two atoms of hydrogen (H_2) with one atom of oxygen (O): its chemical make-up is thus H_2O. Of course, when you turn on a tap, it is not just one molecule coming out but millions!

antiviral, stimulating, decongestant, expectorant.
Slightly irritating to the skin.
e.g.Pinene, Limonene, Camphene.

Sesquiterpenes – end in 'ene' and may have Greek letter prefix

Anti-inflammatory, anti-bacterial, antiseptic, calming, mildly hypotensive, analgesic, antispasmodic.
e.g. Chamazulene, Bisabolene, patchoulene.

Diterpenes

Found in a small number of oils, usually in small quantities, for example sclareol in Clary Sage. Thought to be antiviral, expectorant, antifungal, balancing to endocrine system.

Esters – end in 'yl' and 'ate' or have 'ester' as part of the name

- fungicidal and relaxing.
- sedative
- anti-inflammatory
  e.g. linalyl acetate, benzyl acetate.

Aldehydes – end in 'al' or aldehyde as part of the name

- common in lemon-scented oils
- antiseptic
- sedative
- anti-inflammatory
- can cause skin sensitivity
  e.g. citral in lemongrass

Ketones – end in 'one'

- often poisonous and several oils containing them, e.g. pennyroyal, are banned from use
- decongestants, thus used for upper respiratory problems e.g. thujone (found in clary sage – generally used in preference to sage which has a higher ketone content)
- safe ketones: jasmone (in jasmine) and fenchone (in fennel).

Alcohols – end in 'ol'

- antiseptic, antiviral, uplifting e.g. linalool (in bergamot, basil, ylang ylang); menthol (in peppermint); geraniol (in neroli, geranium, lavender).

Phenols – end in 'ol'

- bactericidal, stimulating e.g. eugenol in basil
- may irritate skin
- most, when isolated, are toxic so it is wise to be extra careful when using any essential oils containing them.

Oxides – end in 'ol' or ole

- expectorant e.g. 1.8 cineole in eucalyptus (globulus, citriodora, smithii, rosemary)
- antibacterial.

Acids – end in 'oic'

- rarely found in essential oils and only in tiny amounts
- anti-inflammatory.

Ethers – normally have 'ether' or 'ethyl'

- anti-depressant
- antispasmodic
- relaxing
  e.g. Methyl chavicol – Basil
- can be neurotoxic.

Lactones – may end in 'ine', 'ene', 'en' or 'one'

- Occur in small amounts in few essential oils
- expectorant
- mucoylytic
- anti inflammatory
- lactones have similar neurotoxic effects to Ketones and may cause skin sensitisation and reactions

Coumarins and Furanocoumarins – end in 'ene'

- calming
- uplifting
- sedative
- hypotenisve
- antispasmodic

e.g. Furanocoumarins such as Bergaptene, found in Bergamot, causes photo-toxicity.

Do synthetic oils have the same effects?

No, because synthetics are rarely exact copies. Most oils are a mixture of two or three chemical elements plus many trace elements (i.e. tiny amounts of other elements). It is the synergy between the main components and the traces, i.e. how all the different molecules work together as a whole oil, which is important. Since exact components of oils are not known, it is impossible to make copies that work as effectively as the real thing.

You now know the basic chemistry of essential oils. This will help you to understand the effect of different oils and make connections between oils from the same plant family with similar molecular structures. The next section explains how aromatherapy works.

HOW ESSENTIAL OILS AND AROMATHERAPY WORK ON THE HUMAN BODY

In order to understand how essential oils work on the body, it is helpful to remember that we are complex chemical beings full of fluids, especially water. It is therefore logical that essential oils, which are also complex chemical fluids, are likely to affect our own body chemistry.

What are the specific effects of aromatherapy?

Using essential oils affects the human body –

- **pharmacologically**: essential oils are chemical and so are humans. Once essential oils have been absorbed into the body, either through the skin or inhalation, the chemicals in the oils enter the blood and other body fluids and interact with the chemistry of our bodies. For example, hormones, enzymes and neurotransmitters (which enable the nervous system to work) are all chemicals and the presence of another chemical (the essential oil) can affect the way they work.
- **physiologically**: physiology is the way our body works. Essential oils can affect this by changing the chemical messages and impulses sent around the body and thus changing the way the systems of the human body function. For example, if an oil has relaxing and de-stressing properties, it may help to relieve the symptoms of stress displayed by our bodies e.g. slowing heart rate and breathing rate or encouraging tense muscles to relax.
- **psychologically**: the way essential oils affect our mind is more difficult to describe, mainly because everyone's mind is different. However, our sense of smell is closely linked to our memory so that particular smells can cause particular responses: for example, if you dislike the smell of roses, rose oil is unlikely to relax you; if jasmine reminds you of a good holiday then its smell will bring back happy memories and provoke a positive response.

The general effects of aromatherapy

There are certain general effects from using essential oils which result from most treatments, especially since relaxing and/or hands-on application methods like massage and baths are very common in aromatherapy. General effects include:

- reduction in stress and tension
- feeling of well-being, balance and calm
- antibacterial effects of oil help the body to heal and support the immune system.

How do essential oils penetrate the body?

There are two ways that oils can safely penetrate the body: smell/inhalation (through the nose) and absorption (through the skin). Ingestion (swallowing them) is considered unsafe and not recommended.

Smelling and inhaling essential oils: the nose and olfactory tract

Smell is the fastest way for essential oils to penetrate the body. The molecules travel up the nose and there are two results: they send a message to the brain and nerves which respond to the new smell and they pass into the bloodstream via the lungs and respiratory system. In order to understand how this works, it helps to understand the structure of the olfactory tract.

Structure

Most of the nose is concerned with breathing: inhaling air into the body and exhaling it from the body. However, it is also the organ of smell and thus very important in a therapy based on the power of aromas! At the top of the nose there are two areas of pigmented tissue known as olfactory membranes. They contain the olfactory, or smell-sensing cells, which have fine hair-like protrusions called cilia. The olfactory cells connect to nerves in an area known as the olfactory plexus. Once triggered, these nerves send messages along the olfactory nerves to the brain, particularly the limbic system. This area of the brain deals with memory, emotions, our basic instincts and mechanical functions.

Function

When the essential oil molecules pass over the olfactory cells, it is thought that these cells trigger receptor areas which send an impulse via the olfactory plexus and nerves to the brain. Here the information is processed and interpreted (i.e. is it a new smell, a nice smell, a smell with positive or negative associations?). Depending on the interpretation, the brain sends messages to other parts of the body to elicit a response (e.g. if dislike is the message the person will stop sniffing the bottle, possibly grimace, and turn away from the smell). The brain may also react to different chemicals in an essential oil and produce particular effects: e.g. a relaxing or sedative substance may cause the brain to send out a message of relaxation either to the whole body or a particular part.

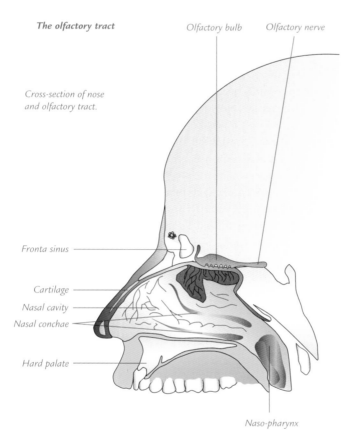

The olfactory tract

Olfactory bulb　*Olfactory nerve*

Cross-section of nose and olfactory tract.

Fronta sinus

Cartilage

Nasal cavity

Nasal conchae

Hard palate

Naso-pharynx

How do oils penetrate the skin?

Essential oils are absorbed through the skin. In order to understand this, it helps to understand the skin's structure. The skin is the largest human organ and it covers the body. It is water-resistant, but extremely minute substances, such as the molecules of an essential oil, can enter the tiny pores of the epidermis, the skin's surface layer, as well as penetrating through the hair follicles and the sweat glands. From the hair follicles and sweat glands, they enter the blood capillaries in the dermis, the skin's second layer. Once the oil reaches the blood and the circulation it is transported around the whole body.

Isn't it faster and thus more effective to swallow oils?

Essential oils should never be swallowed, even when diluted. There are several reasons for this. First, essential oils can be toxic. Second, they are extremely concentrated and, if swallowed, can damage the lining of the stomach. Third, the enzymes in the stomach change the chemical structure of the oils and thus change their therapeutic effect or prevent them from working. Fourth, they put a strain on the liver which works to remove them and fifth they become weaker as they pass through the digestive system.

Finally, it is much slower, not faster, to absorb an oil through the digestive system rather than through the skin or inhalation (where, in both cases, it enters the bloodstream more directly). It is best to think of aromatherapy as an external treatment which has internal effects.

You now know how aromatherapy works and how it affects the body in general. The next section explains the specific benefits and effects of aromatherapy for particular systems of the body.

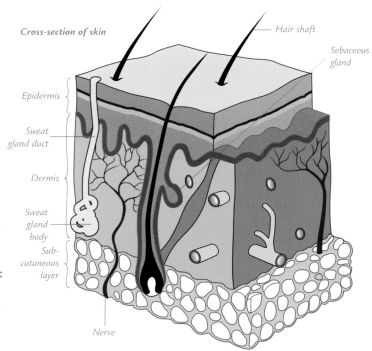

Cross-section of skin

Hair shaft

Sebaceous gland

Epidermis

Sweat gland duct

Dermis

Sweat gland body

Sub-cutaneous layer

Nerve

HOW DO ESSENTIAL OILS AFFECT THE BODY'S INDIVIDUAL SYSTEMS?

Though the effect of a particular oil is generally integral (i.e. applies to the whole body not just one part) it is possible to describe how each system is specifically affected by aromatherapy.

The skin

Aromatherapy massage treatments and baths affect the skin directly because massage involves rubbing oils into the skin and baths involve soaking the skin in water containing oils. So no matter what problem or part of the body is being treated, the skin will benefit, gaining:

- improved circulation through massage bringing fresh nutrients to the tissues and removing waste products.
- improved elasticity which helps to promote healing of scar tissue, reduce stretch marks; increased softness and suppleness
- faster desquamation (the flaking off of

dead skin cells) which encourages the growth of new cells in the basal layer of the dermis as well as promoting a healthier, clearer skin tone.

Treatments for different skin types

Specific essential oil treatments for the skin depend on the problem being treated and/or the skin type. However, since many aromatherapy treatments involve massage of the skin, it is useful to know how to treat different skin types. The five main skin types are combination dry, oily, mature, young and each one benefits from particular oils. Before using any oils, a patch test is recommended: massage a small amount of the prepared essential oil (blended in either a carrier oil or cream) into the crook of the elbow or behind the ear. Leave for 24-48 hours and check for reactions.

Combination Skin

Normally manifests as an oily T panel and dry cheeks and neck. Sufferers may have comedones, open pores, pustules in the oily areas and fine lines and flaking in the dry areas.
For combination skin use:
- Frankincense
- Geranium
- Juniper
- Lavender
- Neroli
- Sandalwood
- Ylang Ylang

Dry

Dry skin suffers from a lack of sebum, a natural oil which is produced by the sebaceous glands in the dermis. It often wrinkles and loses elasticity faster than oily skin. Oils which stimulate the sebaceous glands help to increase the skin's natural lubrication and make the skin more healthy. Dry skin also tends to be sensitive and the oils used for sensitive

skin may also be useful. For dry skin use:
- geranium
- lavender
- sandalwood
- rose
- jasmine
- German chamomile
- Roman chamomile
- neroli.

Oily

In direct contrast to dry skin, oily skin produces too much sebum and is over-lubricated. The most effective treatments use oils that help to control sebum production e.g.
- bergamot
- lavender
- lemon.

In severe cases, oily skin may develop acne. The following oils are beneficial for treating this condition:
- bergamot
- lavender
- geranium
- ylang ylang
- tea tree
- lemongrass
- rosemary.

Mature Skin

Mature skin has lost firmness and elasticity with age making it feel thinner and looser. Changes in texture may cause the appearance of fine lines and less definition in the facial contours. The skin becomes drier and sebaceous gland activity slows. Pigmentation may be patchy due to hormonal changes or sun damage, lymphatic drainage slows leading to puffiness and small capillaries may show through the thinner skin. Mature skin may also have a tendency to sensitivity.
For mature skin use:
- Frankincense
- Geranium
- German Chamomile

- Roman Chamomile
- Jasmine
- Lavender
- Myrrh
- Neroli
- Rose
- Sandalwood

Young Skin

Young skin is even in colour. It has a fine, clear, soft and smooth texture and is supple but firm. The balance of oils and moisture is even.

For young skin use:

- Geranium
- German Chamomile
- Lavender
- Mandarin
- Neroli
- Rose
- Sandalwood
- Ylang Ylang

Skin Conditions

Essential oils/essences are useful for specific skin conditions such as pustules. However, special consideration must be made when treating clients who report skin sensitivity during the consultation process.

Sensitive skin

Sensitive skin is extremely reactive to heat, cold, beauty products and sometimes, massage. Before using any oils on sensitive skin, a patch test is recommended: if there are no abnormal reactions treatment is possible but only using very low concentrations of essential oils. The following oils are all very gentle and suitable for use:

- German Chamomile
- Roman Chamomile
- chamomile
- sandalwood
- neroli
- rose.

The aromatherapist should be especially careful when using absolutes since the solvent used to extract them may cause skin irritation, as residues may remain in the finished essence.

NB Citrus oils may be phototoxic and this should be taken into account when using them to treat the skin.

The vascular system

No matter which method of applying essential oils is used, the essences will eventually find their way into the blood and be transported around the body. Certain essences have a particular effect on the blood and the circulation.

- Hypotensive oils – these oils lower blood pressure and are very efficient for treating high blood pressure (hypertension). They also have calming and relaxing effects, thus reducing blood pressure even further. Hypotensives oils include lavender, marjoram, ylang ylang and lemon.

- Hypertensive oils – low blood pressure is as dangerous as high blood pressure and hypertensive oils help to stimulate and invigorate the circulation, thus increasing pressure and aiding the prevention of other circulatory problems such as chilblains. Hypertensives include rosemary, black pepper, eucalyptus and ginger.

- Tonics – oils with a tonic, cooling effect have an opposite effect to that of rubefacient oils. They help to constrict capillaries thus reducing swellings and inflammations. Tonics include cypress, lemon and clary sage.

- Rubefacient oils – also known as 'warming' oils, these oils warm the tissues in the area of application. This allows the blood vessels in that area to

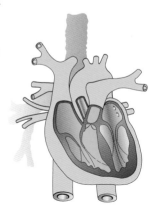

Cross-section of the heart.

HOW AROMATHERAPY WORKS

dilate, enabling a more efficient circulation. Thus the delivery of oxygen and food and the removal of waste are faster which helps to speed up healing. Rubefacients include black pepper, rosemary, ginger, lemon and eucalyptus.

NB Rubefacient oils should not be used on an area that is already red, sore or inflamed.

The skeletal and muscular systems

Joints and muscles benefit from oils with a rubefacient effect. The blood, warmed and stimulated by the oil, moves faster, bringing oxygen to stiff or immobile muscles and joints and thus helping to remove lactic acid build-up and waste such as carbon dioxide. Detoxifying oils, such as juniper, lemon and fennel can help to reduce the uric acid build-up that causes gout as well as relieving the symptoms of arthritis, such as inflammation and swelling. Helpful treatments include:

- rubefacients: black pepper, rosemary, ginger, lemon, eucalyptus.

NB None of these oils should be used on an area that is already red, sore or inflamed.

- depurative (detoxifying): fennel, lemon, juniper, grapefruit.

The lymphatic system

The lymphatic system helps the circulation by collecting any excess tissue fluid that the blood capillaries are unable to carry, filtering it and returning it to the blood. It is especially important for the body's immunity because antibodies and bacteria-eating cells are produced in lymphatic tissue. Stimulating the lymphatic system thus stimulates two processes: the production of antibodies and the filtering of tissue fluid to remove waste and potentially harmful micro-

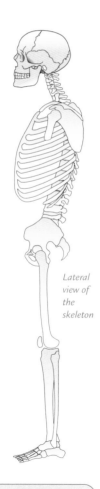

Lateral view of the skeleton

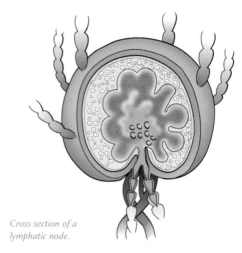

Cross-section of a lymphatic node.

organisms. Oils that stimulate the lymphatic system can be used preventatively, to strengthen the body's own defences or to treat particular conditions caused by an ineffective lymphatic system, like the build-up of cellulite, water retention and bloating. Useful oils include–

- lymphatic stimulants: geranium, juniper, sweet orange
- eliminating oils (for cellulite, bloating): grapefruit, fennel, lemon
- diuretics (for fluid retention): cedarwood, fennel, juniper.

The nervous system

The nervous system is the body's communication and instruction network. Think of it as a very complex wiring arrangement rather like a telephone system linking every area of the body. It is able to send and receive messages to every cell ensuring optimum functioning under all circumstances. It warns the body of danger and sends messages regarding pain and all sensations. Often the nervous system works to protect us by coordinating various body functions and physical and mental reactions. Sometimes a non-physical danger can occur which can produce the sensations of worry or stress. The body has a tendency to react to these sensations in the same way as if a physical danger had occurred, e.g. keeping the body in a state

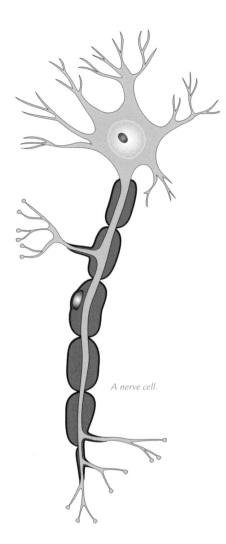

A nerve cell.

of heightened nervousness, anxious and full of adrenaline, ready to react if necessary. In the long term, this can cause tension, restlessness, an inability to relax and insomnia. In more serious cases, high blood pressure and heart problems may develop. Aromatherapy can relax an over-active nervous system and, where pain is felt, slow down the reactions of pain receptors and thus reduce the pain. Useful oils include –

- analgesics: painkillers e.g. German and Roman chamomile, lavender, rosemary
- antispasmodics: calm nerves which tell muscles to go into spasms e.g. German and Roman chamomile, lavender, marjoram

- sedatives: slow down activity thus help relieve insomnia, stress, tension e.g. lavender, German and Roman chamomile, bergamot, ylang ylang
- stimulants: get systems going, for use in cases of convalescence and weakness e.g. basil (used with care), peppermint
- nervines: help the whole nervous system e.g. rosemary, marjoram and neroli.

NB Some oils have a mixture of properties and can be used for several nervous conditions.

The endocrine system

The endocrine system, like the nervous system, is a communication network. It uses chemicals known as hormones to tell the body to grow, change and behave in certain ways. Aromatherapy can help this system in several different ways:

- may help control over/under-production of certain hormones, especially those from the thyroid gland and the adrenal cortex (e.g. basil, geranium and rosemary oils)
- balancing the hormones used in the reproductive system, thus relieving menopausal/menstrual problems e.g. fennel – used with care, clary sage, cypress, German and Roman chamomile, rose, cabbage and damask
- may help control high, and thus potentially dangerous blood sugar levels e.g. geranium, eucalyptus
- may help control appetite e.g. bergamot.

The reproductive system

Essential oils are very useful for treating the problems associated with pre-menstrual tension (depression, anxiety, fluid retention, cramps) and the menopause. However, pregnant women should avoid many essential oils because they are abortifacients (cause abortions) and emmenagogues (provoke menstruation). Helpful treatments include –

- geranium for pre-menstrual tension
- rose, geranium, jasmine for menopausal problems
- jasmine for prostate problems
- chamomile, fennel, juniper, geranium, cypress for fluid retention (PMT)
- rose for re-establishing balance.

NB Essential oils should never be used in the first three months of pregnancy. For the rest of the term, mandarin is the only oil that is recommended for use and only in weak dilution.

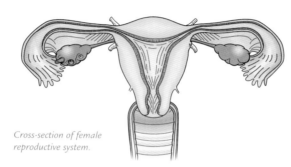

Cross-section of female reproductive system.

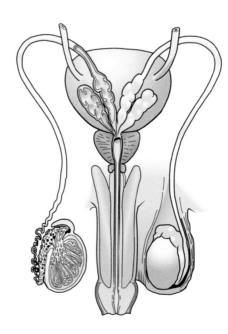

Cross-section of male reproductive system.

The digestive system

Essential oils should not be taken internally but they can be used externally to help the digestive system. Baths and massage of the abdomen both help intestinal problems such as diarrhoea, indigestion and constipation. Also, the inhalation of oils affects the digestive system indirectly because the molecules of essential oils are carried to it in the circulation. Useful oils include –

- antispasmodics (prevent pain and spasm): German and Roman chamomile, clary sage, sweet fennel, peppermint, lavender, petitgrain
- stimulants: black pepper, orange, sweet fennel, ginger, myrrh
- eliminating oils (especially for flatulence): chamomile, fennel, marjoram, peppermint.

The respiratory system

One of the most effective ways of using essential oils is to inhale them, either from a tissue that has been impregnated with drops of oil, in a steam inhalation, from bath water or in the vapours from a burner or diffuser. The essential oil molecules cause impulses to be sent to the brain (see p. 34 'Smelling and inhaling essential oils: the nose and olfactory tract'). The brain can then send responses, which may affect various parts of the body.

The respiratory passages from pharynx to bronchi.

Using essential oils in this way will also allow some of the oil molecules to dissolve in the mucus that lines the respiratory tract. These will then be absorbed into the body's fluids and diffused throughout the body. Many oils have the ability to irritate mucus membranes and a good working knowledge of essential oils is necessary to avoid reactions. It is difficult to do a patch test up the nose!

No matter which method of aromatherapy treatment is used, smelling and breathing in the oils is an important factor. For example, during massage, oils penetrate the skin in a blend or a cream but the smell of the oils used will also have an effect. Thus the respiratory system, like the skin, can benefit directly or indirectly from aromatherapy treatments. Specific treatments to help respiratory problems like asthma, bronchitis, coughs, colds, flu and pneumonia include –

- antispasmodics: bergamot, chamomile, lavender
- decongestants: lavender spike, eucalyptus, globulus and dives
- antiseptics (for infections): bergamot, lavender, eucalyptus, tea tree, lemongrass
- expectorants (encourage coughing and clearing of mucus): cedarwood, eucalyptus, lavender, sandalwood, marjoram
- general cold remedies: eucalyptus, lavender, marjoram, thyme.

The urinary system

The urinary system is the body's liquid waste removal unit. It is often subject to bacterial infections – in the bladder (cystitis), kidneys and urinary tract and aromatherapy can be used to treat the symptoms and effects of these problems. Antiseptic oils can help to clear infections, diuretic oils can be used to encourage urine production and thus help wash away

Above: Cross-section of a kidney.

bacteria and certain oils are effective in relieving the symptoms of kidney infections, although medical advice should be sought before treating any kidney problem. Useful oils include –

- antiseptics: bergamot, German chamomile, tea tree, cedarwood, sandalwood
- diuretics: cypress, fennel, juniper.

The immune system

An immune system that is working properly can help to stop the body becoming ill in the first place. Due to their antiseptic and antiviral qualities, regular use of essential oils can help to strengthen the body's immunity and prevent infection and disease. Most oils have some antibacterial qualities. Oils have two benefits: they can attack bacteria that are already in the body and they can stimulate cells and organs, in a sense waking them up, so that they are better equipped, more efficient and ready to attack any bacteria that appear thus preventing an infection. Useful oils include –

- antibacterial: eucalyptus, tea tree, lavender, myrrh
- antiviral: bergamot, tea tree, rose, marjoram
- febrifuges (reduce fever): eucalyptus, peppermint
- sudorifics (promote sweating): rosemary, peppermint, basil
- overall immune system stimulants: lavender, bergamot, tea tree, thyme, lemon
- lymphatic system stimulants: rosemary, geranium.

You now know all the aspects of aromatherapy function: the chemistry of essential oils and why this is important for oils to work effectively; how oils penetrate the body; the general effects of oils on the whole body and the effect of oils on specific systems.

A cell.

DON'T FORGET TO USE YOUR RESOURCE CD ROM

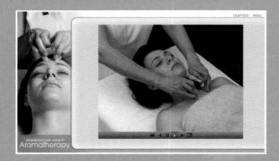

- **TEST YOUR KNOWLEDGE OF ESSENTIAL OILS**

- **TEST YOUR KNOWLEDGE QUESTIONS**

- **FULL VIDEO OF PRACTICAL SKILLS**

AND MUCH MORE!

An introductory guide to Aromatherapy

5 Application: buying and using oils

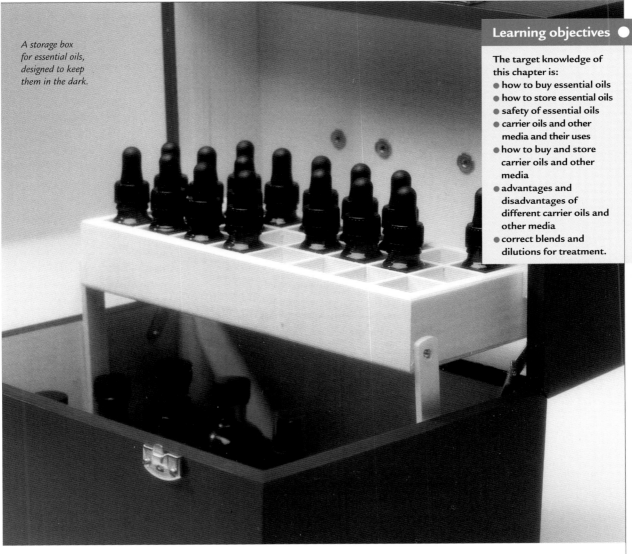

A storage box for essential oils, designed to keep them in the dark.

Learning objectives

The target knowledge of this chapter is:
- how to buy essential oils
- how to store essential oils
- safety of essential oils
- carrier oils and other media and their uses
- how to buy and store carrier oils and other media
- advantages and disadvantages of different carrier oils and other media
- correct blends and dilutions for treatment.

In Brief

This chapter provides information on buying and storing essential and carrier oils and other media, the advantages and disadvantages of using different carrier oils and other media, blending oils for massage and treatments and recommended dilutions.

BUYING AND STORING OILS

Before explaining how to use essential oils it is important to explain how not to use them! The first consideration for anyone planning to use essential oils is where to buy them.

How and where do I buy essential oils?

The most important factor to consider when buying essential oils is who supplies them. With a good, reliable supplier, there is no need to worry about the purity, origin or quality of the oils. The checklist below will help in selecting a supplier: a reputable source will be able to provide all the required information.

- Where is the oil from? What country and which region of that country?
- Was the plant organically grown?
- Which part of the plant was used to produce the oil?
- What is the plant's botanical name (usually in Latin)?
- How was the essential oil extracted: distillation, solvent extraction or expression?
- How long has the oil been in stock?
- Where are the oils stored/are the oils stored properly? (if you are in the shop/warehouse you can check this) i.e. away from extremes of temperature.

Also, be aware of the following –

- are the oils unusually cheap? If so, they might not be the real thing. For example, if rose or jasmine oils are not much more expensive than rosemary or thyme, they might be blends or dilutions...rose and jasmine are extremely expensive.
- buy the best you can afford. The better the quality the better the effect.
- check that the oils are not synthetics, adulterations or 'nature-identical'

copies: the positive effects of an essential oil cannot be exactly synthesised and aromatherapy treatments using artificial or diluted oils will be just as artificial, ineffective and weak!

How should oils be stored?

Essential oils are delicate and expensive. It is therefore wise to look after them. They should be stored –

- away from extremes of temperature: heat will evaporate them and cold can affect their composition
- in dark, amber glass bottles (or dark blue glass bottles if kept in the dark or a refrigerator): essential oils are sensitive to ultraviolet light; they should not be stored, or bought, in plastic because it affects the molecular structure of the oil
- in tightly sealed bottles: to protect them from evaporating in the air and to stop contact with the air from changing their composition
- out of the reach of children (childproof caps are now available for use with essential oil bottles).
- it is important that carrier/fixed oils are also bottled and stored appropriately, away from air, heat and light. They are susceptible to oxidation and hydrolysis – contamination and degradation by oxygen and water and can turn rancid. Changes in the quality of carrier/fixed oils are usually detectable by changes in colour, odour and viscosity.

THE SAFETY OF ESSENTIAL OILS

Are essential oils safe?

Used correctly, essential oils are very safe, mainly because they are used in such tiny amounts. When used in the wrong dilutions and in the wrong conditions they can produce adverse effects. Certain oils should never be used under any circumstances (see list below) and some should not be used for specific conditions.

NB Essential oils are very strong and should not be swallowed. If oil gets into an eye rinse it immediately with lots of water. If necessary seek medical advice.

When should oils not be used?

The effects of certain oils can be positive for some conditions and not for others. Problems can be avoided in three ways:

- consulting with clients to find out as much about their medical history and any contraindications
- knowing the properties and effects of all oils used
- using the oils in their correct and safe dilutions.

General skin irritants

The following oils can irritate the skin so are not recommended for those with sensitive skin or anyone prone to skin allergies. It is also useful to remember that solvent-extracted oils will contain traces of the solvent used and may cause irritations.

Basil	*Melissa*
Black pepper	*Orange*
Clove	*Peppermint*
Ginger	*Thyme*
Lemon	*Tea tree*
Lemongrass	

Photosensitisation

Certain oils make the skin more sensitive to ultraviolet light and should be avoided before exposure to sunlight or before going on a sunbed –

- bergamot
- grapefruit (particularly if distilled)
- lemon
- mandarin
- patchouli
- lime (particularly if expressed)
- sweet orange.

Allergies

For anyone who is allergic or suspects an allergy to a particular oil, a skin test is recommended. Rub one drop of diluted oil into the crook of the arm or behind the ear and leave for 24-48 hours. If there is no reaction, the oil is probably safe to use once diluted as necessary.

Hazards associated with essences:

In addition to irritation and sensitisation, there are other hazards associated with the use of essences. Certain oils are considered to be toxic, causing damage to the body cells and tissues usually through overdoseage or oral ingestion.

Specific conditions

Pregnancy

Avoid oils which have the following properties –

- emmenagogues: provoke menstruation
- diuretics: provoke urine production
- parturients: provoke parturition i.e. childbirth
- abortifacient: cause abortions
- uterine stimulants: cause the uterus to constrict thus provoking abortions.
- The oestrogenic effects of certain oils such as basil and fennel may upset the balance of hormones during pregnancy

NB Essential oils should never be used in the first three months of pregnancy. For the rest of the term, mandarin is the only oil which should be used.

Epilepsy
Never use
- fennel (fenchone)
- rosemary (camphor)

Neurotoxic - can induce seizures.

Liver Disorders
Never use
- fennel (trans-anethole)
- basil (methyl chavicol)

Hepatoxic – can cause damage to liver cells.

Some oils are also suspected of carcinogenisis, forming or stimulating the growth of cancer cells. The oils considered toxic contain many of the chemicals thought to be harmful.

Any medication (prescription and non-prescription) taken must be fully discussed with the client as essences may cause adverse effects when used in combination.

Which oils should never be used?
Here is a list of toxic oils which should never be used, under any circumstances.

Aniseed	*Cinnamon bark*
Arnica	*Dwarf pine*
Bitter almond	*Elecampane*
Bitter fennel	*Horseradish*
Camphor	*Hyssop*
Cassia	*Mustard*
Origanum	
Pennyroyal	
Rue	
Sage	
Sassafras	
Savin	
Savory (winter and summer)	
Southernwood	
Tansy	
Thuja	
Wintergreen	
Wormseed	
Wormwood	

You now know how to buy and store oils and which ones not to buy. The following section explains how to blend them for use.

CARRIER/FIXED OILS & OTHER MEDIA

Essential oils are almost always used in a blend. They are blended with carrier oils for use in massage and, in some cases, baths. The correct blend is very important because essential oils are potentially toxic if used undiluted. They are also highly concentrated and will therefore not go very far in a massage on their own!

What is a carrier oil?
Carrier oils are also known as fixed oils because, unlike essential oils, they do not evaporate when heated. They are extracted from plants, flowers, nuts and seeds. Those generally recommended for use in aromatherapy do not have a strong smell as it might interfere with that of the essential oil. Some carriers contain fat-soluble vitamins (e.g. A, D, E and K), minerals and proteins in different amounts depending on the oil, so some carrier oils have health benefits of their own. Carrier oils used in aromatherapy are –
- of vegetable, nut or seed origin
- refined, extracted using heat and pressure, cold-pressed i.e. they have been extracted without the use of excessive heat which means they are purer and they retain their vitamin content. Some oils are also macerated or infused like calendula.
- stable, not volatile; unlike essential oils they do not evaporate on exposure to heat and light
- used neat

- non-sticky: heat and pressure (massage uses/produces both) can cause some oils to become sticky e.g. avocado; suitable carrier oils are smooth
- lubricants for aromatherapists' hands, giving a smooth massage.

Which oils are recommended?

There are several suitable carrier oils which can be used alone or in a blend with other carriers. Some are lighter than others and often the thicker, denser oils, which are more expensive, are used diluted with a lighter oil to make them go further. Lighter oils are better for full body massage because they allow smoother movements whereas the thicker oils are more useful for massage on a small area.

Recommended carrier oils:

Almond	Macadamia
Apricot kernel	Olive
Avocado	Peach Kernel
Castor	Peanut
Coconut	Sesame
Evening Primrose	Sunflower
Grapeseed	Soya
Hazel	Walnut
Jojoba	Wheatgerm
Linseed	

Almond
(Prunus commmunis)

From the sweet almond nut (not to be confused with bitter almond which is toxic).

Plant family: Rosaceae
Source: Sweet almond nut
Country of origin: Asia, Middle East, and Mediterranean

Properties

- contains high percentage of vitamins (A, B1, B2, B6) and mono- and polyunsaturated fatty acids (essential for the body to function)

- linoleic, oleic, palmitic and linolenic acids
- pale yellow in colour.

Advantages

- keeps well due to vitamin E content
- benefits skin: has protective and nourishing qualities.

Disadvantages

- none

Apricot Kernel
(Prunus armeniaca L.)

Plant Family: Rosaceae
Source: Seed of fruit
Country of Origin: Europe, Asia, Middle East

Properties: light and non-sticky
Advantages: suitable for facial massage, high in vitamins A and E, oleic and linoleic acids, good for all skin types
Disadvantages: May be expensive

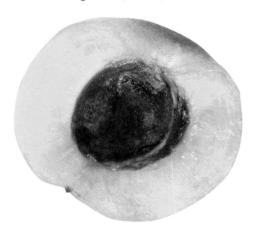

Avocado (Persea Americana)
From avocado fruits.
Plant Family: Lauraceae
Source: Fruit
Country of origin: Central and South America

Properties:
- contains lecithin (which contains phospholipids, which are an important part of all body membranes), saturated and monounsaturated fatty acids (essential for the body to function)
- high vitamin content: A, B, D
- dark green
- high in oleic and palmitic acids, also contains linoleic and linolenic acids

Advantages:
- stores well (because it contains a natural antioxidant)
- emollient (softens and smooths skin)
- good for dry and/or wrinkled skin

- unrefined (which is why, when chilled, the oil sometimes turns cloudy)
- viscous but still penetrates the skin.

Disadvantages:
- can become sticky during massage
- has a strong and distinctive smell.

Castor (Ricinus communis)
Plant family: Euphorbiaceae
Source: Seeds
Country of Origin: Europe, India, China, Brazil

Properties:
- Useful for dry skin and scalp conditions. Used in ointments and compresses. High in Ricinoleic acid. Also contains linoleic, oleic, linolenic and palmitic acids.

Disadvantages:
- May be used in small amounts in blended products as viscous

Coconut (Cocos nucifera)
Plant Family: Arecaceae
Source: Flesh of nut
Country of origin: South Asia, East Indies, USA

Properties:
- High in saturated fats – Caprylic, capric and lauric acids

Advantages:
- Emollient properties make it good for all skin types

Disadvantages:

- Solid at room temperature or heat-extracted, fractionated oil is liquid
- Strong odour
- May cause allergic reactions

Evening primrose (Oenothera biennis)
From evening primrose flower seeds.
Plant family: Onagraceae
Source: Flower seeds
Country of Origin: USA, UK

Properties:
- contains linolenic acid and GLA (gamma-linolenic acid) which are both essential for the body but not made by it so must be provided by diet; GLA is also known to reduce the symptoms of pre-menstrual tension. Also contains oleic and palmitic acids.

Advantages:
- useful for treating dry skin conditions including eczema and dandruff
- useful for PMT.

Disadvantages:
- expensive
- turns rancid quickly if not stored correctly.

Grapeseed (Vitis vinifera)
From the seeds of grapes.
Plant family: Vitaceae
Source: Seeds of grapes
Country of Origin: Mediterranean

Properties:
- finely-textured i.e. smooth, not grainy or sticky, flows freely.
- high in linoleic acid (a poly-unsaturated fatty acid, essential to the body and good for helping prevent heart disease) Also contains linolenic and oleic acids.
- contains some vitamin E (which helps the oil keep for longer and protects/nourishes the skin).

Advantages:
- smooth: good for full body massage
- an inexpensive oil with no odour, it has slightly astringent properties

Disadvantages:
- produced by hot extraction (the raw material is heated beyond 70 degrees to extract the oil), therefore it is not as pure as some other oils.
- May also undergo solvent extraction, thereby increasing the risk of sensitising the skin.

Hazel (Corylus avellana)
Plant family: Corylaceae
Source: Nut
Country of origin: Europe, North America

Properties:
- Light, high in oleic acid, rich in vitamins A, B, E, also contains linoleic, linolenic and palmitic acids, good for oily or combination skin.

Advantages:
- Useful for clients with an oily skin type, acne. Has astringent properties.

Disadvantages:
- May be expensive

Jojoba
(Simmondsia chinensis)
Plant family: Simmondsiaceae
Source: Bean
Country of Origin: USA, Mexico
Jojoba is actually a liquid wax not a carrier oil. It can be a useful addition to a massage oil blend but is too expensive to be used as a base oil.

Properties:
- fine-textured (smooth, not sticky or grainy)
- useful for many conditions: its chemical structure is similar to that of the skin's own oil, sebum, so it is useful for treating both excessive sebum production (oily skin and/or acne) because it can dissolve the sebum, as well as underproduction, such as dry skin, dandruff or other dry skin conditions like eczema and psoriasis
- nourishing
- contains many fatty acids including stearic, erucic, palmitic and palmitoleic acids.

Advantages:
- good for all skin types
- stable (i.e. does not evaporate or react easily with the air) so keeps well.

Disadvantages:
- expensive.

Linseed (Linum usitatissimum)
Plant family: Linaceae
Source: Seeds
Country of Origin: UK, USA, India

Properties: Rich in omega-3 fatty acids – Linolenic acid, oleic and Linoleic acids.

Advantages:
- A rich, healing oil useful for cellulite.

Disadvantages:
- Oxidises rapidly
- May be sticky so blend with other oils

Macadamia
(Macadamia ternifolia)
Plant family: Proteaceae
Source: Macadamia nut
Country of Origin: Australia, Africa

Properties:
- good for dry/wrinkled skin (considered to be anti-ageing)
- emollient
- contains palmitoleic acid, also found in sebum (so therefore useful for treating both dry and oily skins). Also contains oleic, palmitic, stearic and linoleic acids
- golden colour.

Advantages:
- stable
- fine texture.

Disadvantages:
- expensive.

Olive (Olea europaea)
Plant family: Oleaceae
Source: Fruit
Country of Origin: Europe
Properties:
- Emollient, rich in vitamins
- contains oleic, palmitic, linoleic and linolenic acids

Advantages:
- soothes inflamed skin and tissues
- relatively inexpensive

Disadvantages:
- May stain due to chlorophyll content
- may be sticky so useful blended with another fixed oil
- strong odour

Peanut (Arachis hypogaea)
Also known as Arachis or Groundnut oil.
Plant family: Fabaceae (Leguminosae)
Source: Nut
Country of Origin: USA, Australia, Asia

Properties:
- Rich in emollients
- Contains oleic, linoleic, palmitic, archidonic and arachidic fatty acids, vitamin E, magnesium and copper.

Advantages:
- Suitable for dry skin
- inexpensive.

Disadvantages:
- May be sticky, must be avoided with clients with nut allergies

Peach kernel (Prunus vulgaris)
From the stone/seed of peaches.
Plant family: Rosaceae
Source: Stone/seed of the peach
Country of Origin: Mediterranean

Properties:
- similar (in terms of chemical structure and effects) to sweet almond and apricot kernel oils
- light texture, high in vitamins A and E, oleic acid and linoleic acid
- rich in vitamins (A, B1, B2, B6).

Advantages:
- keeps well
- good for all skin types, emollient, anti-inflammatory
- protects and nourishes skin.

Disadvantages:
- expensive.
- almond oil sometimes substituted for Peach kernel – needs careful sourcing.

Sesame (Sesamum indicum)
Plant family: Pedaliaceae
Source: Seeds
Country of Origin: Mediterranean, India

Properties:
- Nourishing, healing
- odour free oil
- easily absorbed by the skin
- High in oleic and linoleic acids, minerals and Vitamin E.
- It also contains linolenic acid.

Advantages:
- It has a natural SPF (Sun protection factor)
- It is healing to dry skin, excema and psoriasis. Good for dry skins.

Disadvantages:
- May be sticky on some skin types

Soya (Glycine max)
Plant family: Fabaceae (Leguminosae)
Source: Soya Bean
Country of Origin: USA, South America, Asia

Properties:
- Not as rich in vitamins as some other oils, does contain a small amount of Vitamin C
- High in linoleic and oleic acids. Also contains palmitic, linolenic, stearic and palmitoleic acids.

Advantages:
- Light, smooth, oil
- suitable for all skin types.

Disadvantages:
- May cause skin reactions, oxidises rapidly

Wheatgerm (Triticum vulgare)

From the vitamin-rich 'germ' (i.e. the seed of the seed which will grow into wheat) of the wheat kernel.

Plant family: Poaceae (Graminae)
Source: Seed of the wheat kernel
Country of Origin: Worldwide

Properties:

- stabilises other oils and blends because it is a natural antioxidant (oxidation is a chemical reaction caused by the presence of oxygen: for example rust is the result of a metal reacting with oxygen and moisture – an antioxidant slows or prevents the reaction and in the case of oils helps to preserve them); adding 5-10% wheatgerm oil to another carrier or a blend will help preserve it for a couple of months
- contains vitamin E and linoleic, palmitic, oleic and linolenic fatty acids
- orangey-brown in colour.

Advantages:

- good for reducing scarring after operations
- useful on dry/mature skins.

Disadvantages:

- too thick and sticky to use alone for massage: needs to be mixed with a light oil
- may cause allergies.

Sunflower (Helianthus annuus)

Plant family: Asteraceae (Compositae)
Source: Seed
Country of Origin: Europe, Africa

Properties:

- Light, non-sticky, rich in vitamins A. B, D and E. Healing to the skin, so useful for treating skin diseases, bruises
- contains linoleic, oleic, palmitic and linolenic acids

Advantages:

- Light
- inexpensive
- good for all skin types

Disadvantages:

- Absorbed slowly, ideally mix with other carriers/fixed oils.

Walnut (Juglans regia)

Plant family: Juglandaceae
Source: Nut
Country of Origin: Europe

Properties:

- Rich in essential fatty acids, emollient - linoleic, oleic, palmitic and stearic acids.

Advantages:

- Normally cold-pressed, so high in nutrients
- Good for dry, ageing or irritated skin

Disadvantages:

- Can sometimes have strong nutty odour
- Use in blends with other oils as it's expensive

APPLICATION: BUYING AND USING OILS

Other Media

Other types of carrier or media may be used to apply the essences in diluted form to the skin or for inhalation via the olfactory tract.

Creams and lotions

Emulsions are a mixture of two or more immiscible (non-mixing) substances, usually water, oil and/or wax, held together by an emulsifier. They are classed as oil-in-water or water-in-oil. Oil-in-water emulsions are lighter – lotions. Water-in-oil products are heavier – creams. Both of these emulsions may be used as bases for the application of essential oils and should be non-perfumed and hypo-allergenic.

Gels

Gels may be natural, such as Aloe vera gel or manufactured from substances such as seaweed. They are non-greasy and therefore useful as carriers where a light application is required. Clients with very oily skins may prefer to home-treat with a gel-based product, or bruised, hot tissue may benefit from the light application of cool gel.

Water

Essences may be used in the bath and with compresses or footbaths as noted in chapter 7.

Air

Burners, vaporisers or diffusers permit the dispersal of oil into the atmosphere, allowing the client to benefit through inhalation.

Clays

These are useful when working with skin conditions. Green, white, pink, yellow and red clays are indicated for use with essences and are particularly useful for oily and disturbed skin conditions. They

can be incorporated into a facial treatment but care must be taken as they can be drying to the skin.

Shea Butter

Botanical Name: Butyrospermum parkii
Source: Nuts from Karite or Shea tree.
Country of Origin: West and Central Africa

Shea butter is a solid fatty oil which is non-toxic. It is anti-inflammatory, healing and easily absorbed. It has a natural SPF and is used in many cosmetics.

Cocoa Butter

Botanical Name: Theobroma cacao
Source: Seeds
Country of Origin: West Africa

Cocoa butter is a solid fat expressed from seeds or beans. It is high in oleic and palmitic acids, Vitamin E and Cocoa Mass Polyphenol (CMP). As an occlusive emollient it can cause irritations to the skin. It has a strong odour.

WHAT IS THE MAXIMUM NUMBER OF OILS PER TREATMENT

Why use a carrier oil?

Carrier or fixed oils are the medium that, literally, carry the essential oil all over the body in a massage. It would be impossible to use essential oils undiluted for massage: they are not only dangerous (because they are so strong) and far too expensive but also ineffective because they are volatile and evaporate with the heat of the massage and in air/light. Carrier oils can slow down the evaporation rate of essential oils and help to transport the essential oil molecules all over the body to be gradually absorbed through the skin. Carrier oils themselves are only absorbed into the surface layers of the skin, because their molecules are too big to penetrate any deeper.

Where should I buy them?

Carrier oils should be bought with the same care as essential oils. Do not make the mistake of using unsuitable oils like cooking oil (think of the aroma and consistency of most cooking oils when used: sticky, greasy and smelly!) or baby oil (this is a mineral oil, not a natural plant oil). Buy from a reputable supplier and, if possible, use oils which are organic and dated (i.e. when they were bottled because shelf lives vary).

How should they be stored?

Remember to –

- replace the bottle lids after use
- store in a cool place: they will go rancid in the heat just like butter left in the sun
- use the oldest first. Carrier oils have a limited shelf life so they need to be used approximately 9-12 months before they go rancid.

What are the correct dilutions?

Dilutions depend on two factors: the treatment and the 'scale' of the treatment (i.e. is it for a full body massage, or just one part such as the face or feet?). The following are guidelines. The more experienced aromatherapist will adapt them according to circumstance and condition. Treat dilutions and blends like a medical treatment: a prescription must provide the right drug and dosage for the condition and patient. The same care should be used to create blends: use the right oils for the problem in the appropriate amounts. For a treatment to work, just like a prescription, the quantities and qualities of both essential and carrier oils must remain consistent.

How much essential oil should be mixed with a carrier oil?

Usually from 1% (weaker blend) to 2% (stronger blend). The maximum dilution should be 2.5% of essential oil.

How do I work out and measure these percentages?

1% equals one drop essential oil to 100 drops carrier and 2% blend equals two drops essential oil to 100 drops carrier.

Do I have to count out 100 drops of a carrier oil?!

No. 100 drops of oil is equivalent to 5mls or one teaspoon. So 1% would be one drop of essential oil per teaspoon/5mls and 2% would be two drops of essential oil per teaspoon/5mls.

How much oil is needed for different treatments?

- Full body massages require about 20-25ml carrier oils. Dilute eight drops essential oil per 20mls carrier.
- For face massage, only about 5mls of carrier oil is needed. Dilute 1-2 drops essential oil per 5ml.
- Absolutes may contain traces of the solvents used in extracting them and thus a weaker dilution such as a 1% blend (i.e. one drop of an absolute to 100 drops/5ml) of carrier oil should be used.
- Baths: essential oils float or sink in water and are not diluted so drops should not be added directly to the water. Oils should be mixed with a small quantity of an emulsifier, such as a fragrance-free shampoo, bath gel, liquid soap or even full cream milk before adding to the bath. No more than six drops should be used per bath. Those with sensitive skin should use a lower concentration and special care should be taken with those essential oils known to cause skin irritations. Essences may also be used in the shower. They can be added to non-fragranced shower gels but care must be taken to select suitable oils for this purpose. 1% dilution recommended. The eye area must be avoided when using the gel.
- Burners/vaporisers: use two drops of the chosen essential oil in water. Diffusers operate by means of an electrical pump. It is important to follow manufacturers instructions and guidance on oils and timings when using this method.
- Compresses: soak cloth in 100ml of water and add one drop of the chosen essential oil.
- Steam inhalations: use one drop of essential oil to a bowl of hot water, or one or two more for a stronger effect.

(See Chapter 7 for more detailed information on using oils at home.)

NB When using essential oils, always be careful not to overdose. If in doubt, don't.

Are there any instances when these dilutions are wrong or need changing?

Use a maximum 1% dilution when treating –

- clients with sensitive skin
- the elderly

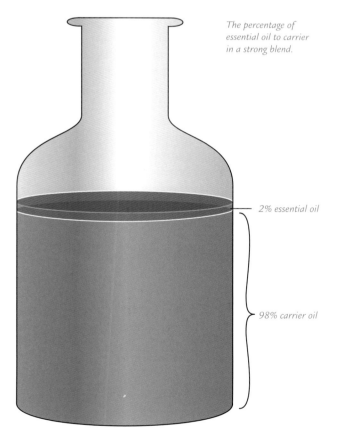

The percentage of essential oil to carrier in a strong blend.

2% essential oil

98% carrier oil

be six months. However, it is best to blend just enough oil for each individual treatment to avoid expense and waste.

Can oils be used undiluted?

Only in very specific circumstances, usually for antiseptic purposes i.e. using a few drops of neat lavender oil on a burn (like Gattefossé, the creator of aromatherapy, did), or dabbing tea tree oil onto a spot or skin blemish. A few drops of particular oils, especially those used for emotional effects like relaxation, stimulation or balance, can be placed onto a tissue and carried around for inhaling when necessary.

What is the maximum number of oils per treatment?

For the treatment of any one person a maximum of three essential oils should be used: two for the body and one for the face when required. Obviously, oils will mix in the body but certain oils are specifically recommended for treating skin types. No treatment should use more than eight drops of essential oil.

Does the treatment start working immediately?

The smell of an oil during any treatment will register in the brain and provoke a response within seconds. In massage, essential oils are primarily absorbed through the skin, and then into the body fluids. An area of skin is only able to absorb oils for about ten minutes after which it becomes saturated. The time taken for the oils to pass around the body is dictated by the individual metabolic rate and this varies from about twenty minutes to twelve hours. Most essential oils are processed and eliminated from the body within 24 hours although there are a few exceptions e.g. juniper and myrrh which both remain in the body for longer and therefore require careful use.

- children
- the weak/convalescent
- pregnant or breastfeeding women.

In general, blends should be adapted according to the strength of the smell of the essential oils used as well as the age and condition of the client. The amount of oil that needs to be blended is obviously dictated by the physical size of the client and which areas are being massaged. Someone with a larger frame will have more skin to massage! However, the dilution of the blend should never exceed 2.5%.

How long will the blend last?

The average shelf life of a blended oil, provided that the carrier oil is fresh, is approximately three months. If 10% of wheatgerm oil, a natural antioxidant, is added to the blend the shelf life should

Blending

Blending is a complicated art at first – there are many oils to choose from and a potentially confusing array of client requirements, which can often seem daunting for the therapist. It is best to select between one and three oils for a blend. Using the client consultation, decide upon the presenting conditions. The client's skin type may also provide an opportunity to select specific oils. Decide upon the emphasis of the blend – for example is it stress, insomnia or backache the client is having problems with? Select the appropriate oil based upon chemistry, therapeutic properties and the client's scent preferences. Clients often have favourite scents and may not always like the most relevant or useful oils for their condition. Select up to three essences in this way, taking into account any other conditions and approach the treatment in a holistic way, thinking about the physical and psychological needs of the client. Carrier/fixed oils will also need to be considered as part of an effective blend. Essences chosen may overlap conditions being treated and a synergistic effect may be created. Once the client is happy with the chosen oils, the therapist can create the blend using the correct dilutions (as detailed previously). Record the specific blending ratios, quantities of oils used, oil details, including botanical names and reasons for choice on the client consultation form for future reference and reflective practice.

The client must also sign the consultation form to endorse the blend chosen.

Fragrance Notes

The note of an essential oil may help provide some guidance when creating a blend. A technique of classification developed by the perfume industry, essential oils are categorised by their volatility - the rate at which they evaporate.

Top notes

These evaporate quickly and may be the first scents noticed in a blend. Examples include Basil, Bergamot and Eucalyptus.

Middle Notes

These have a slower rate of evaporation and are often used to balance a blend. Examples include Black pepper, peppermint and Sweet Marjoram.

Base notes

These notes evaporate slowly and their scent develops over time. Some base notes can be overpowering so the aromatherapist needs to use them with care. Examples include Patchouli, Frankincense and Jasmine.

This is not a definitive science as some oils fall into two or more note categories. An experienced nose will develop with time and blending skills will increase as the therapist gains practical experience and confidence.

Oils that are blended for the client following a thorough consultation should be appropriately bottled and labelled. The label should contain the client's name, date that the blend was created, a 'use by date', the common and Latin names of the essences and fixed oils blended, directions for use i.e., once per day, the name and contact details of the therapist, safety precautions to be followed i.e., not to be used in the bath, not to be applied before sun exposure.

6 A-Z of essential oils

In Brief
The next chapter provides an easy reference guide to 42 of the most important essential oils.

A–Z OF ESSENTIAL OILS

● A–Z EXPLAINED

Now that you have learnt what essential oils are and how to use them, you need to learn about the properties and effects of each individual oil. The oils are listed in alphabetical order.

Each listing includes the following –

● **common name** the name used generally for an oil/essence

● **botanical name** (useful for double-checking that what is contained in a bottle of oil is the real thing, not a substitute).

● **plant family:** plants are classified into specific botanical groups – normally identified by similar structure and growing habits

● **where** the plant comes from.

● which **part of the plant** is used for the oil (some plants produce several oils).

● **method of extraction**: useful because methods like solvent extraction leave a residue which can irritate the skin.

● **chemical make-up**: when you first encounter essential oils, their chemical make-up can be very confusing and difficult to understand. It may even seem irrelevant. However, gradually patterns begin to emerge and the different chemical constituents become recognisable. In a way it's a bit like a recipe: if something contains yeast it will rise, if it contains chilli it will be spicy, if it

contains lots of sugar it will be sweet and if it contains lots of salt it will be salty. The same applies to the 'ingredients' of essential oils. So if you know that an oil contains a high proportion of terpenes, which are antiviral, stimulating and antiseptic, then you will know that the oil has these qualities. Or if an oil contains a high proportion of alcohols, which are antiseptic and uplifting, the oil itself will be antiseptic and uplifting. Also, once you know that one plant from a particular group contains terpenes, alcohols or esters, and has the qualities connected with those chemicals, it is likely that another plant from that group will have a similar chemical make-up and effects. For example, most citrus oils contain a high proportion of a terpene called limonene. Terpenes are antiviral, antiseptic and invigorate the body so all citrus oils will have strong antiseptic and invigorating qualities. Indeed, any oil containing limonene will have those effects to a greater or lesser extent depending on the proportion it contains.

In each entry the main chemical constituent is listed.

● **therapeutic actions**: the effects of the oil on the body. You will notice that some oils are listed with apparently contradictory actions (for example stimulating and relaxing). This is because they have such complex chemical compositions that one molecule may act in one way on the body

whereas another may cause a completely opposite reaction. However, this does not mean that a treatment used for relaxation will be cancelled out by itself. An oil's molecules will be stimulated by the oils it is mixed with and how it is applied/used; these will determine the final outcome of the treatment. These oils are known as adaptogens.

● **conditions and systems that benefit from using the oil**: these list conditions that the oil has been shown to help but they are not meant to be exclusive. Experimenting (taking into account any safety factors or contraindications) with oils and blends is the best way to find out what works best for each individual. Reflective practice and case study work help the therapist to record and identify the effects of individual oils or blends and their success in treatment.

● **safety factors**: contraindications to an oil's use are listed here. It should be noted that very few oils are recommended for use during pregnancy and that epileptics, those with blood pressure problems or sensitive skin should take extra care.

● **if you remember only one thing...**: though it is impossible to sum up the benefits of any one oil, this last section gives a thumbnail description of its positive qualities.

GLOSSARY OF THERAPEUTIC ACTIONS

- **Analgesic**: painkilling effect
- **Anti-acid**: reduces the effects caused by too much gastric acid
- **Anti-allergic**: prevents allergic reactions
- **Anticatarrhal**: helps remove catarrh
- **Antidepressant**: helps lift depression and symptoms related to it
- **Anti-inflammatory**: reduces inflammations
- **Antimicrobial**: an agent which resists or destroys pathogenic micro-organisms
- **Antipruritic**: relieves sensation of itching or prevents its occurrence
- **Antiseptic**: prevents or removes infection
- **Antispasmodic**: calms, slows muscle spasm
- **Antiviral**: kills virus, or helps prevent a virus developing
- **Aphrodisiac**: heightens sexual desire
- **Astringent**: contracts and tightens tissues, especially skin
- **Bactericidal**: kills bacteria
- **Balancing**: creates balance in emotions or in activity of part of the body
- **Calming**: has an overall calming effect
- **Carminative**: helps prevent flatulence
- **Cephalic**: clears and focuses the mind
- **Cicatrisant**: helps wounds heal
- **Cooling**: cools the area of application; reduces temperature
- **Cordial**: a stimulant and tonic
- **Cytophylactic**: cell-regenerator
- **Deodorant**: removes or masks unpleasant smells
- **Depurative**: removes impurities and toxins
- **Diuretic**: increases urine production
- **Emmenagogue**: provokes menstruation – useful for clients suffering from amenorrhoea (absence of periods) but contraindicated for pregnant women
- **Expectorant**: helps fluidify, thus remove, mucus from lungs and respiratory passages
- **Febrifuge**: reduces fever
- **Fungicidal**: destroys fungi
- **Galactagogue**: increases the secretion of breast milk
- **Haemostatic**: stops bleeding
- **Hypertensive**: increases blood pressure
- **Hypotensive**: lowers blood pressure
- **Immuno-stimulant**: stimulates the immune system
- **Laxative**: promotes evacuation of the bowel
- **Nervine**: strengthening and toning to the nerves and nervous system
- **Oestrogenic**: helps promote production of oestrogen
- **Prophylactic**: preventive of disease or infection
- **Relaxing**: has a general relaxing effect
- **Refreshing**: has a refreshing effect
- **Rubefacient**: warms and reddens the area of application, and subsequently the blood vessels in that area dilate
- **Sedative**: calms the nervous system
- **Stimulant**: stimulates a particular system or the whole body
- **Stomachic**: aids digestion, eases indigestion
- **Sudorific**: increases perspiration
- **Tonic**: invigorates and gives strength to a specific area or the whole body depending on the oil
- **Uplifting**: helps positive thinking, 'lifts' the emotions
- **Vasoconstrictive**: reduces dilation of capillaries (thus reducing blood flow to an area and the redness it causes)
- **Vasodilatory**: increases dilation of capillaries (thus warming and increasing the blood flow to an area causing it to redden)
- **Vermifuge**: expels intestinal worms
- **Vulnerary**: An agent which helps heal wounds and sores by external application
- **Warming**: produces feeling of warmth.

Basil

One of the best herbs for cooking, basil is also a versatile essential oil.

What is its botanical name?
Ocimum basilicum.

Which plant family does it come from?
Lamiaceae (Labiatae)

Where in the world does it come from?
Basil originates in Asia and Africa but is now found throughout the Mediterranean area of Europe (Italy and France) and in the USA.

Which part of the plant is used to make the oil?
The flowers and leaves of the herb.

How is it extracted?
By steam distillation.

What is its chemical make up?
Basil may consist of linalool (Alcohol), eugenol, methyl chavicol, limonene and citronellol
NB Basil with a low methyl chavicol and eugenol content should be used where possible as these are potential sensitisers

What are its general therapeutic actions?

Basil has the following actions:
- antiseptic
- antispasmodic
- cephalic
- emmenagogue
- tonic
- uplifting
- warming
- prophylactic.

Which conditions/systems benefit from using basil oil?
- *skin*: tonic effect on acne; reduces inflammation of wasp stings
- *muscular/digestive*: antispasmodic; relieves muscle tightness, especially in the intestines and stomach
- *nervous*: uplifting for depression, insomnia, stress; helps to focus the mind and aids concentration; headaches, migraine, fainting fits, neuralgia, neuritis
- *reproductive*: amenorrhoea (absence of periods) or irregular/scanty menstruation
- *respiratory*: sinusitis.

When shouldn't it be used?
On sensitive skins and pregnant women.

If you remember only one thing...
Basil is excellent for clearing the mind of worries and clutter
and lifting one's spirit.

Benzoin

What is its botanical name?
Styrax benzoin.

Which plant family does it come from?
Styracaceae

Where in the world does it come from?
Sumatra, Java and Thailand.

Which part of the plant is used to make the oil?
The resin of the benzoin tree.

How is it extracted?
By solvent extraction

What is its chemical make up?
Benzoin may consist of coniferyl cinnamate (Ester) and sumaresinolic acid, combined with benzoic acid and traces of cinnamic acid, vanillin and benzaldehyde.

What are its therapeutic actions?
Benzoin has the following actions:
- carminative
- expectorant
- sedative
- cordial
- vulnerary
- warming.

Which conditions/systems benefit from its use?
- *skin*: reduces inflammations and relieves symptoms of dermatitis, cracked and chapped skin
- *skeletal*: warming effect reduces inflammation caused by rheumatoid arthritis and gout
- *circulatory*: warms heart and circulation and thus improves their efficiency
- *nervous*: stress, relieves tension
- *digestive*: aids digestion and relieves flatulence
- *urinary*: cystitis.

When shouldn't it be used?
Benzoin is relatively safe for use, though sensitive skins may react to it.

If you remember only one thing...
Benzoin creates a feeling of euphoria, and has a warming effect on the whole body, especially the heart, lungs and circulation.

Did you know?
Benzoin oil was once used in a product called Friar's Balsam, an inhalation used to ease respiratory problems.

Bergamot

What is its botanical name?
Citrus bergamia.

Which plant family does it come from?
Rutaceae

Where in the world does it come from?
It is native to tropical Asia but now cultivated in northern and southern Italy.

Which part of the plant is used to make the oil?
The rind/peel of the bergamot fruit, which resembles a miniature orange.

How is it extracted?
By expression.

What is its chemical make up?
Bergamot may consist of linalyl acetate (Ester), and linalool

What are its therapeutic actions?
Bergamot has the following actions:
- analgesic
- antiseptic
- antiviral
- cooling
- relaxing
- sedative
- laxative
- vermifuge
- uplifting.

Which conditions/systems benefit from its use?
- *skin*: antiseptic, thus useful for treating many skin conditions such as eczema, psoriasis and acne
- *nervous*: uplifting thus reduces anger, frustration, anxiety, stress and the symptoms of depression
- *digestive*: relieves flatulence, colic and painful digestion; helps regulate appetite
- *respiratory*: relieves symptoms of colds,

flu and bronchitis as well as reducing inflammations and infections such as tonsillitis and sore throats
- *urinary*: cystitis
- *immune*: strengthens system.

When shouldn't it be used?
Before going into the sun or onto a sunbed since it increases sensitivity to ultraviolet light.
NB: Bergaptene-free bergamot should be used where possible because bergaptene is a furocoumarin which is the phototoxic ingredient.

If you remember only one thing...
Like other citrus oils bergamot is uplifting and cheerful.

● **Did you know?**

Bergamot oil used to be a common ingredient in suncreams and oils. They all had a distinctive, orangey scent.

Cedarwood Atlas

What is its botanical name?
Cedrus atlantica

Which plant family does it come from?
Pinaceae

Where in the world does it come from?
Algeria and Morocco

Which part of the plant is used to make the oil?
Wood stumps or sawdust

How is the oil extracted?
By steam distillation

What is its chemical make up?
Cedarwood may consist of atlantone (ketone), cedrol , cedrene, caryophyllene, cadinene

What are its therapeutic actions?
- Antiseptic
- Antifungal
- Antiseborrhoeic
- Astringent
- Diuretic
- Expectorant
- Mucoylitic
- Nervine
- Sedative
- Tonic

Which conditions/systems benefit from its use?
- Skin: dandruff, seborrhoea of scalp, acne, oily skin
- Muscular: Aches and pains, stiffness
- Nervous: Reduces anxiety, tension and stress
- Urinary: Cystitis and urinary tract infections
- Lymphatic system: Cellulite and oedema
- Respiratory: coughs, colds, catarrh, bronchitis

When shouldn't it be used?
Cedarwood atlas should not be used during pregnancy, however it is generally non-toxic and non-irritating.

If you remember only one thing...
Cedarwood atlas is useful for respiratory problems, and suitable for men as the odour is woody and sweet.

Chamomile (German)

This type is also known as blue chamomile.

What is its botanical name?
Matricaria recutita

Which plant family does it come from?
Asteraceae (Compositae)

Where in the world does it come from?
Europe, specifically Hungary and Bulgaria although it is still grown and exported from Germany.

Which part of the plant is used to make the oil?
The flowers.

How is it extracted?
Steam distillation.

What is its chemical make-up?
German chamomile may consist of bisabolenes (sesquiterpene) and chamazulene (which is a product of the distillation process but does not exist in the flower)

What are its therapeutic actions?
German chamomile is
- analgesic
- anti-allergic
- anti-inflammatory
- antispasmodic
- emmenagogue (mild)
- sedative (nervous system)
- stimulant (immune system)
- vulnerary
- vermifuge.

Which conditions/systems benefit from its use?
- *skin*: calms and soothes many skin conditions, especially allergies, bruises, eczema, blisters, acne, psoriasis and ulcers
- *skeletal*: eases aching joints and infant teething pains, arthritis
- *muscular*: relieves muscular pain
- *nervous*: relaxes thus relieving anxiety, tension and insomnia
- *reproductive*: antispasmodic so relieves period pain; also relieves symptoms of PMT and menopause
- *digestive*: regulates peristalsis thus relieving irritable bowel syndrome; relieves indigestion and nausea
- *immune*: stimulates whole system.

When shouldn't it be used?
In the early stages of pregnancy.
Some very sensitive skins may react to it so a skin test should be performed prior to use.

If you remember only one thing...
Chamomile is very versatile, calming and relaxing, good for children (especially if hyperactive), the frail and the elderly.

Chamomile (Roman)

What is its botanical name?
Chamaemelum nobile

Which plant family does it come from?
Asteraceae (Compositae)

Where in the world does it come from?
Europe, especially England, Belgium, France and the USA.

Which part of the plant is used to make the oil?
The flowers.

How is the oil extracted?
By steam distillation.

What is its chemical make-up?
Roman chamomile may consist of 2-methylbutyl (Ester), isobutyl angelate, angelic and tiglic acids, pinocarvone and chamazulene.

What are its therapeutic actions?
Roman chamomile is

- analgesic
- anti-inflammatory
- antiseptic
- antispasmodic
- bactericidal
- emmenagogue
- sedative (nervous system)
- stomachic
- vulnerary
- vermifuge
- tonic.

Which conditions/systems benefit from its use?

- *skin*: rashes, allergies, dry skin conditions; effective for eczema, psoriasis
- *skeletal*: soothes joint inflammations, arthritis
- *muscular*: soothes inflammations, aches and pains
- *nervous*: stress, depression, insomnia, relaxing thus reduces tension and anxiety
- *digestive*: teeth abscesses, diarrhoea, nausea, upset stomach, nervous indigestion
- *reproductive*: premenstrual tension and fluid retention; relieves period pain and menopausal depression
- *urinary*: cystitis and other urinary tract infections.

When shouldn't it be used?
Non-toxic, non-irritant, non-sensitising; however may cause reactions in some individuals - skin patch test prior to use. No known contraindications and is good for use with children.

If you remember only one thing...
Roman chamomile, like the German variety, is calming and effective and a good all-round oil.

Clary sage

What is its botanical name?
Salvia sclarea.

Which plant family does it come from?
Lamiaceae (Labiatae)

Where in the world does it come from?
England, Russia, Morocco, France, Italy, Spain.

Which part of the plant is used to make the oil?
The leaves and flowers.

How is it extracted?
Steam distillation.

What is its chemical make-up?
Clary sage may consist of linalyl acetate (Ester), linalool, pinene and myrcene.

What are its therapeutic actions?
Clary sage is
- anti-inflammatory
- antispasmodic
- relaxing
- sedative
- tonic
- uplifting
- hypotensive oil

Which conditions/systems benefit from its use?
- *skin*: reduces inflammations, oily skin
- *muscular*: relaxes muscles, reduces spasm, muscle fatigue, cramp, fibrositis
- *nervous*: uplifts and promotes feeling of well-being/euphoria, soothes nervous tension, panic and acts as a sedative, relieves headache and migraine symptoms
- *respiratory*: antispasmodic properties ease symptoms of asthma
- *reproductive/endocrine*: balances hormones, relieves PMT, fluid retention and painful cramps, menopausal symptoms
- *immune*: general tonic strengthens the immune system making it useful for the weak/convalescent.

When shouldn't it be used?
During pregnancy and before or after drinking alcohol (the oil can increase the effects of drunkenness).
Non-toxic, non-irritant, non-sensitising

If you remember only one thing...
Clary sage is warming, relaxing and uplifting.

Cypress

What is its botanical name?

Cupressus sempervirens.

Which plant family does it come from?

Cupressaceae

Where in the world does it come from?

Mediterranean countries such as France, Spain, Italy, Portugal; also parts of North Africa.

Which part of the plant is used to make the oil?

Leaves/needles and cones (like small fruits).

How is it extracted?

Steam distillation.

What is its chemical make-up?

Cypress may consist of α-pinene (monoterpene), camphene plus other trace molecules like sabinol.

What are its therapeutic actions?

Cypress is

- antispasmodic
- astringent
- haemostatic
- diuretic
- tonic
- uplifting
- vasoconstrictive.

Which conditions/systems benefit from its use?

- *cells and tissues of whole body*: astringent; acts as a diuretic, acts on cellulite and water retention
- *skin*: controls water loss, oil and sweat production; good for excessive perspiration, oily and mature skins
- *circulatory*: narrows blood vessels so eases varicose veins, haemorrhoids and heavy bleeding
- *reproductive*: regulates problems related to menstruation (heavy periods, PMT, hormonal and menopausal problems).

When shouldn't it be used?

Generally safe and non-irritating.

If you remember only one thing...

Cypress is a strong astringent so it controls the body's production of liquids (excess sweat or oil, fluid retention, heavy menstrual bleeding).

Eucalyptus globulus

There are several types of eucalyptus so check the botanical name of the oil purchased/used to ensure it is the one you want.

What is its botanical name?
Eucalyptus globulus.

Which plant family does it come from?
Myrtaceae.

Where in the world does it come from?
The eucalyptus tree is a native of Tasmania and Australia but it is now grown in Mediterranean countries like Spain and Portugal.

Which part of the plant is used to make the oil?
The leaves and twigs of the tree.

How is it extracted?
Steam distillation.

What is its chemical make-up?
Eucalyptus globulus may consist of 1-8 cineole (Oxide), limonene and α-pinene

What are its therapeutic actions?
Eucalyptus globulus is
- analgesic
- antiseptic
- antispasmodic
- antiviral
- depurative
- expectorant
- prophylactic
- stimulant
- uplifting.

Which conditions/systems benefit from its use?
- *skin*: infections and dull, congested skin, burns, wounds, outbreaks of spots
- *skeletal*: eases rheumatism
- *muscular*: relieves aches and pains
- *nervous*: clears the head, calms emotions, headaches
- *respiratory*: effective for all cold and flu symptoms as well as throat infections, catarrh, sinusitis, asthma, infections, coughs (expectorant – clears mucus by encouraging coughs)
- *urinary*: cystitis
- *immune*: stimulates body's immunity against infection.

When shouldn't it be used?
Eucalyptus globulus should only be used in low dilutions since it may irritate the skin. It is incompatible with homeopathic treatments.
Eucalyptus oil is toxic if taken internally.

If you remember only one thing...
Eucalyptus globulus protects the whole body against disease and viruses by strengthening the immune system.

THIS IS
EUCALYPTUS

Eucalyptus citriodora

What is its botanical name?
Eucalyptus citriodora

Which plant family does it come from?
Myrtaceae

Where in the world does it come from?
Australia, South America, South Africa

Which part of the plant is used to make the oil?
The leaves

How is it extracted?
Steam distillation

What is its chemical make-up?
Eucalyptus citriodora may consist of citronellal (aldehyde), citronellol, geraniol and pinene

What are its therapeutic actions?
Eucalyptus citriodora is

- antiseptic
- antiviral
- bactericidal
- expectorant
- stimulant
- uplifting
- insect repellent

Which conditions/systems benefit from its use?

- skin: fungal infections, herpes, dandruff, insect repellent
- respiratory: asthma, throat infections
- immune: colds, influenza, infections

When shouldn't it be used?
Non-toxic, non-sensitising, non-irritant but a skin test is required for sensitive skins Not compatible with homeopathic remedies. Eucalyptus oil is toxic if taken internally.

If you remember only one thing...
Lemon-scented Eucalyptus citriodora is a good insect repellent

A–Z OF ESSENTIAL OILS

THIS IS
EUCALYPTUS

Eucalyptus dives

What is its botanical name?
Eucalyptus dives

Which plant family does it come from?
Myrtaceae

Where in the world does it come from?
Australia and South Africa

Which part of the plant is used to make the oil?
The leaves

How is it extracted?
Steam distillation

What is its chemical make-up?
Eucalyptus dives may consist of pipertone (ketone), α-phellandrene, viridiflorol, terpinen-4-ol and other compounds

What are its therapeutic actions?
Eucalyptus dives is
- antiseptic
- analgesic
- antiviral
- antifungal
- decongestant
- expectorant
- mucoylitic
- rubefacient
- stimulant
- uplifting

Which conditions/systems benefit from its use?
- skin: fungal infections, wounds, sores
- skeletal: arthritis, rheumatism
- muscular: aches and pains, sporting injuries,
- nervous: headaches, migraines,
- respiratory: asthma, throat infections, bronchitis, coughs, catarrh
- immune: colds, influenza, infectious illnesses

When shouldn't it be used?
Non-toxic, non-sensitising, non-irritant. Not compatible with homeopathic remedies. Eucalyptus oil is toxic if taken internally.

If you remember only one thing...
Mint-scented Eucalyptus dives is good for respiratory conditions

Eucalyptus smithii

What is its botanical name?
Eucalyptus smithii

Which plant family does it come from?
Myrtaceae

Where in the world does it come from?
South Africa and Australia

Which part of the plant is used to make the oil?
The leaves

How is it extracted?
Steam distillation

What is its chemical make-up?
Eucalyptus smithii may consist of 1-8 cineole (Oxide), limonene, globulol, - α-pinene, and other compounds

What are its therapeutic actions?
Eucalyptus smithii is
- antiseptic
- analgesic
- antiviral
- antibacterial
- decongestant
- expectorant
- rubefacient
- stimulant
- uplifting

Which conditions/systems benefit from its use?
- skin: acne, boils, infections
- skeletal: arthritis, rheumatism
- muscular: aches and pains,
- nervous: headaches, migraines
- respiratory: asthma, throat infections, bronchitis, coughs, catarrh
- immune: colds, influenza, infectious illnesses

When shouldn't it be used?
Non-toxic, non-sensitising, non-irritant but a skin test is required for sensitive skins Not compatible with homeopathic remedies. Eucalyptus oil is toxic if taken internally.

If you remember only one thing...
Suitable for children and the elderly, Eucalyptus smithii is good for skin infections and respiratory conditions

THIS IS
EUCALYPTUS

● **Did you know?**

Sweet fennel is one of the main ingredients in babies' gripe water.

Fennel

It is important to distinguish between sweet fennel and bitter fennel. Sweet fennel is widely used in aromatherapy but bitter fennel is considered too toxic.

What is its botanical name?
Foeniculum vulgare.

Which plant family does it come from?
Apiaceae (Umbelliferae)

Where in the world does it come from?
Mediterranean countries such as France, Italy and Greece.

Which part of the plant is used to make the oil?
The crushed seeds.

How is it extracted?
Steam distillation.

What is its chemical make-up?
Sweet fennel may consist of methyl chavicol (Phenolic ether) trans-anethole, limonene, pinene, and phellandrene.

What are its therapeutic actions?
Sweet fennel is
- antiseptic
- antispasmodic
- carminative
- depurative
- diuretic
- galactagogue
- emmenagogue
- laxative
- antimicrobial
- tonic.

Which conditions/ systems benefit from its use?
- *skin*: clears congestion; antiseptic qualities help bruises to heal and relieve pain and irritation from bites and stings
- *skeletal*: helps rheumatism

- *circulatory*: helps reduce cellulite
- *lymphatic*: oedema, eliminates toxins
- *digestive*: eases spasms in digestive tract, relieves colic, flatulence, constipation
- *reproductive*: eases PMT, amenorrhoea and menopausal problems; increases milk flow in nursing mothers
- *urinary*: cleanses kidneys and stimulates them
- *general*: detoxifies the body; good for hangovers.

When shouldn't it be used?
During pregnancy, for epileptics and in large doses (which can be narcotic). Otherwise, it is generally non-toxic and safe to use on the skin.
NB Sweet fennel should never be confused with bitter fennel which is not recommended for use.

If you remember only one thing...
Fennel cleans out the body. It is a natural diuretic and depurative, so it helps to get rid of cellulite, flatulence, water retention or constipation.

Frankincense

What is its botanical name?
Boswellia sacra.

Which plant family does it come from?
Burseraceae

Where in the world does it come from?
Frankincense, as might be obvious from its Biblical associations, comes from a tree or shrub which grows in the Red Sea region. It now also grows in Africa, especially the north-east, Somalia and Ethiopia.

Which part of the plant is used to make the oil?
The resin of the tree or shrub.

How is it extracted?
Steam distillation.

What is its chemical make-up?
Frankincense may consist of α-pinene (monoterpene) and limonene plus trace molecules

What are its therapeutic actions?
Frankincense is
- emmenagogue
- expectorant
- relaxing
- rubefacient
- sedative
- tonic

Which conditions/systems benefit from its use?
- *skin*: rejuvenates mature skins by smoothing wrinkles and dry skins; balances oily skins
- *nervous*: comforting, warming, relaxing; burn (in a burner) during meditation to help focus the mind, stress, anxiety
- *respiratory*: helps asthma, bronchitis, coughs, laryngitis; clears mucus and catarrh; calms breathing
- *urinary*: eases symptoms of cystitis
- *reproductive*: dysmenhorrhea, metrorrhagia

When shouldn't it be used?
Frankincense is non-toxic and non-irritant.

If you remember only one thing…
Frankincense is emotionally balancing, producing a sense of calm.

Geranium

What is its botanical name?
Pelargonium graveolens

Which plant family does it come from?
Geraniaceae

Where in the world does it come from?
Geranium plants are originally natives of South Africa but are now grown worldwide, especially in Mediterranean Europe, Russia and Egypt.

Which part of the plant is used to make the oil?
The whole plant contains the essential oil so most of it is used: the leaves, flowers and flower stalks.

How is it extracted?
Steam distillation.

What is its chemical make-up?
Geranium may consist of geraniol (Alcohol), citronellol and linalool, with traces of limonene and menthone

What are its therapeutic actions?
Geranium is
- astringent
- antidepressant
- diuretic
- anti-inflammatory
- balancing
- haemostatic
- vulnerary
- vermifuge
- stimulant
- tonic
- uplifting.

Which conditions/systems benefit from its use?
- *skin*: benefits all skin types, balances sebum, helps keep skin supple, tonifies dull, congested skins, improves circulation thus preventing chilblains and enlivening pale skin, bruises, eczema, broken capillaries
- *circulatory/lymphatic*: improves circulation and stimulates lymphatic system, odema, cellulite
- *nervous*: tonic, lifts the spirits and relieves anxiety, depression and stress
- *endocrine/reproductive*: balances the hormones, thus regulating PMT, menopause (especially the depression associated with this), and heavy periods.

When shouldn't it be used?
On very sensitive skin. Otherwise it is completely safe.

If you remember only one thing...
Geranium balances both mind and body, is emotionally uplifting and stimulates the circulation.

Ginger

What is its botanical name?
Zingiber officinale.

Which plant family does it come from?
Zingiberaceae

Where in the world does it come from?
Asia (especially India), tropical countries (especially Jamaica and the West Indies) and Nigeria.

Which part of the plant is used to make the oil?
The thick, horizontal root of the plant, known as a rhizome. These are dried and ground.

How is it extracted?
By steam distillation.

What is its chemical make-up?
Ginger may consist of Zingiberene (Sesquiterpene), zingiberol, gingerol, gingerone plus traces of camphene and citronellal

What are its therapeutic actions?
Ginger is
- stimulating
- tonic
- analgesic
- laxative
- warming
- rubefacient
- antispasmodic
- analgesic
- stomachic.

Which conditions/systems benefit from its use?
- *skin*: stimulates circulation thus helps heal bruises and chilblains
- *skeletal*: eases joint pain, arthritis and rheumatoid arthritis
- *muscular*: relieves cramps, muscle spasms and sprains
- *circulatory*: stimulates the circulation which helps to ease blood vessel problems such as varicose veins, warming to cold hands and feet
- *nervous*: warms emotions, especially when lethargic and fatigued
- *digestive*: settles the stomach, nausea, motion sickness, stimulates appetite
- *respiratory*: eases flu and cold symptoms, especially catarrh, sore throats, fever, runny nose
- *general*: removes toxins, stimulates and wakes up body.

When shouldn't it be used?
On very sensitive skins as it can be phototoxic. Ginger is spicy and can thus be an irritant. It should only be used in low concentrations.

If you remember only one thing...
Ginger is spicy and warm. It stimulates the circulation and wakes up sluggish, tired bodies. It also calms and settles the stomach.

Grapefruit

What is its botanical name?
Citrus paradisi.

Which plant family does it come from?
Rutaceae

Where in the world does it come from?
Tropical Asia, the West Indies, USA.

Which part of the plant is used to make the oil?
The fruit peel.

How is it extracted?
Expression.

What is its chemical make-up?
Grapefruit may consist of limonene (monoterpene) plus cadinene, paradisiol, neral

What are its therapeutic actions?
Grapefruit is
- astringent
- depurative
- diuretic
- stimulant
- tonic
- uplifting.

Which conditions/systems benefit from its use?
- *skin*: astringent for dull, oily skin and acne
- *lymphatic*: diuretic thus reduces water retention and oedema, helps cellulite
- *nervous*: uplifting and refreshing thus revives depressed and stressed minds,
- *immune*: stimulates immunity and helps to prevent colds and flu
- *general*: fatigue, jet-lag, morning tiredness.

When shouldn't it be used?
Grapefruit is safe and not an irritant. Also, unlike other citrus oils, it is only phototoxic when distilled. However, if the extraction method is not known it should be treated as phototoxic.

If you remember only one thing...
Grapefruit is a refreshing tonic and has an uplifting effect, thus helps combat depression (especially S.A.D.), lethargy and general fatigue.

Jasmine

What is its botanical name?
Jasminum grandiflorum.

Which plant family does it come from?
Oleaceae

Where in the world does it come from?
China, northern India, Egypt, France and many Mediterranean countries.

Which part of the plant is used to make the oil?
The flowers.

How is it extracted?
A concrete is produced by solvent extraction; further solvent extraction creates an absolute which may then be steam distilled to produce the essential oil. The traditional method (and the most expensive) is enfleurage.

What is its chemical make-up?
Jasmine may consist of benzyl acetate (Ester), linalool, jasmone, α & β -pinene

What are its therapeutic actions?
Jasmine is
- antidepressant
- antispasmodic
- galactagogue
- parturient
- relaxing
- sedative
- tonic (uterine).

Which conditions/systems benefit from its use?
- *skin*: encourages cell renewal thus heals scar tissues and reduces stretch marks; hydrates and soothes dry, mature skin and increases elasticity
- *nervous*: improves self-confidence, optimism, lifts depression, calms nerves and warms emotions; eases nerve pain

- *reproductive/endocrine*: balances hormones in PMT and menopause; eases child labour pains and speeds up delivery.

When shouldn't it be used?
Jasmine is useful at the end of pregnancy, because it strengthens uterine contractions, but it is thus not recommended for use during pregnancy.

If you remember only one thing...
Jasmine rejuvenates the skin and the soul, relaxes, soothes and uplifts.

80

● Did you know?

Gin gets its flavour from juniper berries.

Juniper (berry)

What is its botanical name?
Juniperus communis.

Which plant family does it come from?
Cupressaceae

Where in the world does it come from?
Juniper naturally grows in the north, particularly Siberia, Canada and in Scandinavian countries. However, the oil is mainly produced in France, Italy, Hungary, the Czech Republic and Slovakia.

Which part of the plant is used to make the oil?
The best oil comes from the dried berries but a cheaper oil is made from the needles and wood of the tree.
NB Only juniper berry oil is recommended for use in aromatherapy.

How is it extracted?
By steam distillation.

What is its chemical make-up?
Juniper may consist of α & β pinene (monoterpenes), limonene, myrcene and sabinene

What are its therapeutic actions?
Juniper is
- antiseptic
- antispasmodic
- depurative
- diuretic
- emmenagogue
- relaxing
- sedative
- stimulant
- tonic
- warming
- rubefacient.

Which conditions/systems benefit from its use?
- *skin*: detoxifies blocked pores, acne, oily skin; good for dermatitis, psoriasis and eczema
- *skeletal*: warming effect eases symptoms of arthritis, rheumatism and gout
- *circulatory*: aids cellulite
- *nervous*: clears and stimulates the mind, relieves stress-related conditions and tension
- *urinary*: cystitis; diuretic helps fluid retention.

When shouldn't it be used?
Juniper is an abortifacient (stimulates the uterus muscles) so it should never be used during pregnancy. It may also irritate the kidneys and should not be used on those with kidney disease or on those who have ever suffered from nephritis. Prolonged use can cause kidney damage.

If you remember only one thing...
Juniper detoxifies, cleaning out the body and mind of excesses, whether fluids, anxieties or the build-up of toxins.

Lavandin

A hybrid plant from a cross of true lavender and lavender spike.

What is its botanical name?
Lavandula x intermedia

Which plant family does it come from?
Lamiaceae (Labiatae)

Where in the world does it come from?
The Mediterranean, but cultivated worldwide

Which part of the plant is used to make the oil?
The flowers

How is it extracted?
Steam distillation

What is its chemical make up?
Lavandin may consist of linalyl acetate (Ester), linalool 1-8 cineole, borneol, lavendulol, terpinen -4-ol.

What are its therapeutic actions?
Lavandin is:

- antispasmodic
- analgesic
- antimicrobial
- mucolytic
- insecticide

Which conditions/systems benefit from its use?

- skin: insect repellent
- circulatory: palpitations
- digestive: stimulates the appetite, soothes colic, flatulence
- respiratory: infections, colds, flu
- muscular: soothes aches and pains, antispasmodic
- nervous: stimulating and uplifting

When shouldn't it be used?
Non-toxic, non-irritating, non-sensitising.

If you remember only one thing...
Lavandin is commonly used to adulterate other oils, particularly Lavandula angustifolia. Inexpensive and suitable for use in burners and vaporisers, particularly for respiratory conditions.

Lavender (true)

Lavender is a good oil to learn with because it is very versatile and inexpensive.

What is its botanical name?
Lavandula angustifolia.

Which plant family does it come from?
Lamiaceae (Labiatae)

Where in the world does it come from?
Mediterranean countries, especially France, and England.

Which part of the plant is used to make the oil?
The flowers.

How is it extracted?
By steam distillation.

What is its chemical make-up?
Lavender has too many constituents to list (more than 100). However, the main one is linalool (alcohol), linalyl acetate (Ester), lavandulyl acetate and lavandulol

What are its therapeutic actions?
Lavender is
- analgesic
- anti-inflammatory
- antiseptic
- antispasmodic
- antiviral
- balancing
- cooling
- detoxifying
- fungicidal
- hypotensive
- relaxing
- sedative
- tonic

Which conditions/systems benefit from its use?
- *skin*: effective for use on all skin types and conditions – balances sebum in oily skin, promotes cell growth and rapid healing for scars and stretch marks, antiseptic for insect bites and stings, burns, sunburns, wounds, healing for dermatitis and psoriasis
- *skeletal*: eases rheumatism
- *muscular*: soothes and relieves aches, pains and sprains
- *circulatory*: lowers high blood pressure and other stress-related conditions such as palpitations
- *nervous*: balances emotions, lifts depression, relieves stress, insomnia and anxiety; relieves headaches, migraine, tension, shock
- *respiratory*: relaxes breathing, eases bronchitis, laryngitis; antiviral effect on flu and colds.

When shouldn't it be used?
Lavender is neither toxic nor irritating.

If you remember only one thing...
The whole body can benefit from lavender. It is an all-rounder, useful for treating all conditions as well as relaxing and balancing the whole body.

IMAGE SHOWS
LAVENDER NOT
LAVENDER SPIKE

Did you know?

During the Great Plague judges carried lavender bags and sprigs of lavender were used to pack gloves. Apparently, neither judges nor glove-packers contracted the disease!

Lavender, spike

What is its botanical name?
Lavandula latifolia

Which plant family does it come from?
Lamiaceae (Labiatae)

Where in the world does it come from?
The Mediterranean, particularly France and Spain

Which part of the plant is used to make the oil?
The flowers

How is it extracted?
Steam distillation

What is its chemical make up?
Lavender, spike may consist of 1-8 cineole (oxide), linalool, camphor and borneol plus terpenes

What are its therapeutic actions?
Lavender, spike is:

- analgesic
- expectorant
- mucolytic
- insecticide
- vulnery
- uplifting

Which conditions/systems benefit from its use?
- *skin:* insect repellent
- *muscular/skeletal:* aches and pains, rheumatism
- *nervous:* headaches
- *respiratory:* Cold, flu, and catarrh

When shouldn't it be used?
Lavender, spike is non-toxic, non-irritant, non-sensitising. However, use in low concentration, as the camphor content is considered neurotoxic

If you remember only one thing...
Lavender, spike is an uplifting oil useful for aches and pains

Lemon

What is its botanical name?
Citrus limon.

Which plant family does it come from?
Rutaceae

Where in the world does it come from?
Lemon trees are cultivated all over the world. They are native to Asia and India and also grow wild in Mediterranean countries such as Spain and Portugal.

Which part of the plant is used to make the oil?
The fresh peel (zest) of the fruit.

How is it extracted?
Expression.

What is its chemical make-up?
Lemon may consist of limonene (Monoterpene), α & β pinene, plus cintronellol and citral

What are its therapeutic actions?
Lemon is
- antiseptic
- antiviral
- detoxifying
- depurative
- diuretic
- fungicidal
- haemostatic
- hypotensive
- stimulant
- tonic
- uplifting.

Which conditions/systems benefit from its use?
- *skin*: useful for boils, warts, acne/other seborrhoeic conditions
- *circulatory*: tonifies blood and improves circulation, reduces pressure on varicose veins, lowers high blood pressure, slows external bleeding including nosebleeds
- *nervous*: refreshes and stimulates the mind, allowing clarity of thought
- *digestive*: dyspepsia
- *respiratory*: protects against infections like colds and flu, lowers temperature
- *immune*: stimulates immune system to produce protective white blood cells.

When shouldn't it be used?
Do not use if going into the sun. Lemon oil is phototoxic and may cause sensitivity to sunlight. It may irritate skin and should thus be used in low concentrations.

If you remember only one thing...
Lemon protects and stimulates the body's systems and lifts the emotions.

Lemongrass

Lemongrass is an important ingredient in Thai cuisine, and the oil, like the plant has a lemony and spicy quality.

What is its botanical name?
Cymbopogon citratus.

Which plant family does it come from?
Poaceae (Gramineae)

Where in the world does it come from?
Lemongrass grows in Asia, in the West Indies and East India.

Which part of the plant is used to make the oil?
The leaves of the grass (both fresh and part-dried).

How is it extracted?
By steam distillation.

What is its chemical make-up?
Lemongrass may consist of citral (Aldehyde), citronellal, geraniol plus traces of other compounds such as limonene and myrcene

What are its therapeutic actions?
Lemongrass is
- antidepressant
- antiseptic
- astringent
- stimulant
- tonic
- uplifting.

Which conditions/systems benefit from its use?
- *skin*: tonifies open pores, acne, oily skin; insect-repellent
- *skeletal*: useful for aching joints, gout, rheumatism
- *muscular*: tonifies aching muscles, tired legs and veins, relieves muscle fatigue; useful for sports injuries
- *nervous*: stimulates, revives, energises the emotions and relieves stress-related conditions and nervous exhaustion
- *digestive*: stimulates appetite, relieves indigestion and gastro-enteritis
- *respiratory*: antiseptic effect on infections, sore throats, laryngitis
- *immune system*: reduces fever.

When shouldn't it be used?
Lemongrass is non-toxic but may irritate the skin.

If you remember only one thing...
Lemongrass is refreshing and stimulating for muscles and skin.

Mandarin

Mandarin is a member of the citrus family. It is known as tangerine in North America.

What is its botanical name?
Citrus reticulata.

Which plant family does it come from?
Rutaceae

Where in the world does it come from?
Southern China and Eastern Asia.

Which part of the plant is used to make the oil?
The peel of the fruit.

How is it extracted?
Expression.

What is its chemical make-up?
Mandarin consists mainly of limonene (Monoterpene), α & β pinene plus methyl methyl-anthrilate, geraniol and citral

What are its therapeutic actions?
Mandarin is
- antiviral
- carminative
- relaxing
- antispasmodic
- tonic
- sedative
- uplifting.

Which conditions/systems benefit from its use?
- *skin*: helps cell growth for scar tissue and stretch marks; astringent for oily skin
- *lymphatic*: mild diuretic qualities help cellulite, oedema
- *nervous*: mandarin's refreshing aroma

lifts anxiety and symptoms of depression as well as helping insomniacs
- *reproductive*: helps PMT
- *digestive*: tonifies digestion, expels wind, calms the stomach and stimulates appetite.

When shouldn't it be used?
It can be mildly phototoxic if used before exposure to sunlight.

If you remember only one thing...
Mandarin is refreshing and happy, soothing and relaxing and eases all aspects of nervous exhaustion and anxiety. It is useful for treating children and the frail or elderly and is the only oil considered safe for use after the first trimester of pregnancy.

Marjoram (sweet)

What is its botanical name?

Origanum majorana.

Where in the world does it come from?

Mediterranean countries such as Spain, France and Egypt; also parts of North Africa.

Which plant family does it come from?

Lamiaceae (Labiatae)

Which part of the plant is used to make the oil?

Dried flowers and leaves.

How is it extracted?

By steam distillation.

What is its chemical make-up?

Marjoram may consist of terpinen-4-ol (Alcohol), linalool, terpinene, sabinene, geranyl acetate and linalyl acetate

What are its therapeutic actions?

Marjoram is

- analgesic
- antispasmodic
- emmenagogue
- relaxing
- sedative
- tonic
- nervine
- laxative
- vulnerary
- vasodilatory
- warming
- hypotensive.

Which conditions/systems benefit from its use?

- *skin*: helps heal bruises
- *skeletal*: eases joint problems
- *muscular*: eases aches and pains, especially after sport, also helps period cramps

- *circulatory*: lowers high blood pressure, improves poor circulation and prevents chilblains
- *nervous*: calms and soothes the emotions, especially in times of stress, grief and loneliness; good for headaches, insomnia and migraines
- *digestive*: eases stomach cramps, indigestion and constipation
- *respiratory*: eases congestion in nose and sinuses, relieves asthma and bronchitis.

When shouldn't it be used?

Marjoram is an emmenagogue and should not be used during pregnancy.

If you remember only one thing...

Marjoram is a soothing and comforting oil, which calms over-active minds, warms the body and relieves anxiety and distress.

Myrrh

What is its botanical name?
Commiphora myrrha.

Which plant family does it come from?
Burseraceae

Where in the world does it come from?
Red Sea area and North-east Africa (Ethiopia, Sudan); South-west Asia.

Which part of the plant is used to make the oil?
The resin of the myrrh shrub or tree.

How is it extracted?
A resinoid is extracted by solvent extraction and an essential oil by steam distillation.

What is its chemical make-up?
Myrrh may consist of heerabolene (Sesquiterpene), cuminyl alcohol, limonene and cinnamaldehyde

What are its therapeutic actions?
Myrrh is
- anticatarrhal
- anti-inflammatory
- antiseptic
- carminative
- cicatrisant
- cooling
- emmenagogue
- expectorant
- fungicidal
- sedative
- vulnerary
- stimulant (digestive, pulmonary)
- tonic.

Which conditions/systems benefit from its use?
- *skin*: chapped skin, fungus infections like athlete's foot and ringworm, wounds; good for mature skins

- *nervous*: stimulates and revives, relieving apathy, lack of motivation and general lethargy
- *reproductive*: regulates menstrual cycle; relieves thrush
- *digestive*: mouth and gum ulcers, gingivitis; stimulates appetite, aids diarrhoea, flatulence
- *respiratory*: myrrh is good for helping all respiratory problems; anticatarrhal and expectorant thus helps remove mucus from lungs; antiseptic and anti-inflammatory thus good for all infections, colds, bronchitis and glandular fever.

When shouldn't it be used?
Myrrh is not recommended for use during pregnancy or in high concentration.
NB It takes more than 24 hours to eliminate myrrh from the body and thus it should not be used on a regular or prolonged basis.

If you remember only one thing...
Myrrh is a healer, especially good for healing wounds, mouth and gum problems and infections of the respiratory system.

Neroli (Orange blossom)

What is its botanical name?
Citrus aurantium

Which plant family does it come from?
Rutaceae

Where in the world does it come from?
Mediterranean countries (Italy, France, Spain), parts of North Africa and China.

Which part of the plant is used to make the oil?
Orange blossom flowers.

How is it extracted?
Solvent extraction or steam distillation.

What is its chemical make-up?
Neroli may consist of α-terpineol (Alcohol), linalool, limonene and linalyl acetate

What are its therapeutic actions?
Neroli is
- antidepressant
- antispasmodic
- cicatrisant
- detoxifying
- relaxing
- sedative
- tonic
- uplifting.

Which conditions/systems benefit from its use?
- *skin*: helps cell regeneration (tonic) thus benefiting dry, mature skins, scars and stretch marks, thread veins, eczema and psoriasis
- *circulatory*: tonic for circulation (especially varicose veins) and eases palpitations (due to calming effect)
- *nervous*: lifts depression, relieves stress-related conditions, especially insomnia, and anxiety; eases neuralgia, calms and soothes nerves and nerve endings
- *reproductive*: relieves PMT.

When shouldn't it be used?
Neroli is not known to have any contraindications.

If you remember only one thing...
Neroli is a tonic for the nervous system. It rejuvenates body and soul!

Orange (bitter)

What is its botanical name?
Citrus aurantium

Which plant family does it come from?
Rutaceae

Where in the world does it come from?
The Mediterranean, USA, South America

Which part of the plant is used to make the oil?
The peel of the fruit

How is it extracted?
Expression

What is its chemical make up?
Orange bitter may consist of limonene (monoterpene), myrcene, camphene, pinene and other compounds

What are its therapeutic actions?
Orange bitter is:

- astringent
- antiseptic
- anti-inflammatory
- sedative
- tonic
- carminative

Which conditions/systems benefit from its use?

- *skin*: Oily, congested skins
- *circulatory*: water retention, palpitations
- *nervous*: stress, nervous tension, and tension headaches
- *respiratory*: bronchitis
- *immune*: colds, flu

When shouldn't it be used?
Orange bitter is non-toxic, non-irritant, non-sensitising. It should not be used before going into the sun as it is phototoxic.

If you remember only one thing...
A bright, sunny oil – orange bitter is a tonic to the nervous system and useful for stress related conditions.

Orange (sweet)

What is its botanical name?
Citrus sinensis.

Which plant family does it come from?
Rutaceae

Where in the world does it come from?
The sweet orange is native to China but is extensively grown in California, Florida and Mediterranean countries (such as Spain, France, Italy).

Which part of the plant is used to make the oil?
The peel of the fruit.

How is it extracted?
Expression or steam distillation, but the distilled oil is a poorer quality.

What is its chemical make-up?
Sweet orange may consist of limonene (Monoterpene), pinene, myrcene and other compounds

What are its therapeutic actions?
Sweet orange is
- antidepressant
- antispasmodic
- antiviral
- hypotensive
- sedative
- stimulant (digestive, lymphatic)
- stomachic
- uplifting.

Which conditions/systems benefit from its use?
- *skin*: skin tonic for dull, oily skins; refreshes and detoxifies
- *circulatory*: hypotensive thus lowers blood pressure
- *lymphatic*: relieves oedema and fluid retention
- *nervous*: provokes positive outlook, refreshes the mind, lifts and relieves depression, tension and stress
- *digestive*: calms the stomach, aids peristalsis, helps relieve digestive problems such as diarrhoea and constipation
- *immune*: helps protect against infections, colds and flu.

When shouldn't it be used?
Expressed sweet orange oil is safe but the distilled version causes phototoxicity (sensitivity to sunlight).

If you remember only one thing…
Sweet orange is a member of the citrus family. These fruits only grow naturally in sunny hot countries and the oils from them are like a burst of sunshine: uplifting, warm, bright, restorative.

● **Did you know?**

Patchouli was a very
popular perfume in
the 1960s.

Patchouli

What is its botanical name?
Pogostemon cablin.

Which plant family does it come from?
Lamiaceae (Labiatae)

Where in the world does it come from?
Asia: Philippines, Indonesia, Malaysia,
China, India.

**Which part of the plant is used to make
the oil?**
The dried leaves.

How is it extracted?
Steam distillation.

What is its chemical make-up?
Patchouli is mostly α & β patchoulene
(Sesquiterpenes) and patchoulol

What are its therapeutic actions?
Patchouli is
- antidepressant
- anti-inflammatory
- cytophylactic
- diuretic
- fungicidal
- sedative
- tonic
- antimicrobial
- nervine
- prophylactic
- uplifting.

**Which conditions/systems benefit from
its use?**
- *skin*: helps cell growth, scarred tissue,
  chapped skin; insect repellent
- *nervous system*: relieves stress-related
  conditions, lethargy, anxiety
- *digestive*: stimulant; helps peristalsis,
  aids weight loss.

When shouldn't it be used?
Patchouli should be used in low
concentrations since it may cause
phototoxicity.

If you remember only one thing...
Patchouli is both uplifting and sedative:
a small amount stimulates the nervous
system; a large amount is relaxing and
soothing.

Which part of the plant is used to make the oil?
The dried berries.

How is it extracted?
By steam distillation.

What is its chemical make-up?
Black pepper may consist of α & β pinene (Monoterpene), α & β phellandrene, camphene, limonene and thujene

What are its therapeutic actions?
Black pepper is
- analgesic
- antispasmodic
- rubefacient
- tonic
- stomachic.

Which conditions/systems benefit from its use?
- *muscular*: tonic for aches and pains; can improve performance if used before sporting activities
- *circulatory/lymphatic*: warming thus stimulates circulation (thus preventing and relieving chilblains) and lymphatic system
- *nervous*: stimulates and thus strengthens the nerves and mind
- *digestive*: stimulates digestion and appetite; relieves bowel problems and constipation by aiding peristalsis
- *respiratory*: catarrh, coughs and colds.

When shouldn't it be used?
Black pepper can be irritating and should not be used neat on the skin. It is also incompatible with homeopathic treatments. Use in low concentrations

If you remember only one thing...
Black pepper warms the blood, thus relieving aches and pains in the muscles and stimulating the appetite.

Pepper (black)

The black pepper we use on our food isn't quite the same as the essential oil; however, the oil does have the same spicy quality and can therefore be a skin irritant.

What is its botanical name?
Piper nigrum.

Which plant family does it come from?
Piperaceae

Where in the world does it come from?
India, Indonesia, Greece.

Peppermint

What is its botanical name?
Mentha piperita.

Which plant family does it come from?
Lamiaceae (Labiatae)

Where in the world does it come from?
Grown worldwide, most peppermint oil now comes from the USA.

Which part of the plant is used to make the oil?
The leaves and flowers.

How is it extracted?
Steam distillation.

What is its chemical make-up?
Peppermint may consist of menthol (Alcohol), menthone, menthyl acetate, limonene and pulegone

What are its therapeutic actions?
Peppermint is
- analgesic
- antiseptic
- antispasmodic
- antiviral
- antipruritic
- carminative
- cephalic
- cooling
- digestive tonic
- expectorant
- febrifuge
- stimulant
- stomachic
- vermifuge
- uplifting
- vasoconstrictive.

Which conditions/systems benefit from its use?
- *skin*: vasoconstrictor thus reduces inflammations, itching; cooling effect on sunburn, hot flushes
- *nervous*: wakes up and refreshes the mind, improves concentration, helps mental fatigue, headaches and depression; cools and calms anger, hysteria, nervous trembling
- *digestive*: effective for flatulence, indigestion, nausea, travel sickness
- *respiratory*: decongests blocked sinuses, relieves asthma, cold and flu symptoms; encourages perspiration thus reducing fever
- *general*: relieves pain and cools – headaches, migraines, toothache, aching feet.

When shouldn't it be used?
Peppermint counteracts the benefits of homeopathic remedies and should not be used with, or even stored near them. It should also be avoided late in the day and by insomniacs since it refreshes the mind, waking you up!

If you remember only one thing...
Peppermint is cool, refreshing and good for the digestion.

Petitgrain

What is its botanical name?
Citrus aurantium.

Which plant family does it come from?
Rutaceae

Where in the world does it come from?
Mediterranean countries, especially France, parts of North Africa; Paraguay.

Which part of the plant is used to make the oil?
The leaves and twigs.

How is it extracted?
By steam distillation.

What is its chemical make-up?
Petitgrain may consist of linalyl acetate (Ester), geranyl acetate, linalool, terpineol, and geraniol

What are its therapeutic actions?
Petitgrain is
- antidepressant
- antiseptic
- antispasmodic
- digestive
- relaxing
- stimulant (digestive, nervous)
- nervine
- tonic
- uplifting.

Which conditions/systems benefit from its use?
- *skin*: tonic for greasy skin and hair
- *nervous*: soothes anxiety, tension, hyper-activity; sedates nervous spasms and physical problems relating to this such as rapid heartbeat and breathing, insomnia, fatigue
- *digestive*: calms stomach muscles, relieves indigestion, upset stomach and painful digestion
- *immune*: mild stimulant, which helps body recover after illness.

When shouldn't it be used?
Petitgrain has no known ill-effects.

If you remember only one thing...
Petitgrain is a great stress-reliever and anti-depressant.

Rose (cabbage)

Cabbage rose is sometimes known as French rose. Distilled rose oil is known as rose otto.

What is its botanical name?
Rosa centifolia.

Which plant family does it come from?
Rosaceae

Where in the world does it come from?
Morocco, France, Italy and Tunisia. It is also grown in China.

Which part of the plant is used to make the oil?
The flower petals.

How is it extracted?
The best oil comes from direct/steam distillation. However, a lot of rose oil is solvent extracted, producing a concrete and then absolute.

What is its chemical make-up?
Cabbage rose may consist of citronellol (Alcohol), geraniol, nerol, phenyl ethanol, and stearoptene

What are its therapeutic actions?
Cabbage rose is
- antidepressant
- antiseptic
- antispasmodic
- antiviral
- astringent
- bactericidal
- depurative
- emmenagogue
- haemostatic
- relaxing
- sedative
- laxative
- tonic
- vulnery.

Which conditions/systems benefit from its use?
- *skin*: anti-inflammatory, tonic and astringent effect on broken capillaries and thread veins; dry, mature skin and wrinkles; eczema
- *nervous*: rose oil is a very effective anti-depressant and also helps relieve symptoms of nervous tension and stress as well as insomnia; stimulates positive emotions, thus combating jealousy, sadness, grief; balancing
- *reproductive*: regulates menstrual problems and uterine disorders, calms PMT, increases semen production; relaxing thus helps impotence/ frigidity.

When shouldn't it be used?
Rose cabbage is non-toxic, non-irritant, non-sensitising and has no known contraindications.

If you remember only one thing...
Cabbage and damask rose have very similar properties but cabbage rose is said to be more aphrodisiac and more relaxing than damask.

Rose (damask)

Damask rose (sometimes known as Bulgarian rose), like jasmine, is one of the best and the most expensive of essential oils. However, it can be used sparingly to great effect so it may be worth the investment. Distilled rose oil is known as rose otto.

What is its botanical name?
Rosa damascena.

Which plant family does it come from?
Rosaceae

Where in the world does it come from?
Rosa damascena is native to Asia but is mostly cultivated in Bulgaria, Turkey and France.

Which part of the plant is used to make the oil?
The flower petals.

How is it extracted?
The best oil comes from water/steam distillation. However, a lot of rose oil is solvent extracted, producing a concrete and then absolute.

What is its chemical make-up?
Damask rose may consist of citronellol (Alcohol), geraniol, nerol, stearoptene and a small amount of phenylethyl alcohol

What are its therapeutic actions?
Damask rose is
- antidepressant
- antiseptic
- antispasmodic
- antiviral
- astringent
- bactericidal
- cicatrisant
- depurative
- emmenagogue
- haemostatic

- relaxing
- sedative
- laxative
- tonic.

Which conditions/systems benefit from its use?
- *skin*: anti-inflammatory, tonic and astringent effect on broken capillaries and thread veins; dry, mature skin and wrinkles; eczema
- *nervous*: rose oil is a very effective antidepressant and also helps relieve symptoms of nervous tension and stress as well as insomnia; stimulates positive emotions, thus combating jealousy, sadness, grief; balancing
- *reproductive*: regulates menstrual problems and uterine disorders, calms PMT, increases semen production; relaxing thus helps impotence/frigidity.

When shouldn't it be used?
Rose damask is non-toxic non-irritant, non-sensitising and has no known contraindications.

If you remember only one thing...
Damask rose is especially effective for emotional and reproductive problems. It is also said to be an aphrodisiac...!

A–Z OF ESSENTIAL OILS

Rosemary

Rosemary is from the same plant family as lavender and, like its relative, it has many uses in aromatherapy.

What is its botanical name?
Rosmarinus officinalis.

Which plant family does it come from?
Lamiaceae (Labiatae)

Where in the world does it come from?
Rosemary grows all over the world but it comes mainly from Mediterranean countries such as France, Spain and Italy.

Which part of the plant is used to make the oil?
The leaves and flowers of the herb.

How is it extracted?
By steam distillation.

What is its chemical make-up?
Rosemary is made up of α & β pinene (Monoterpenes), 1-8 cineole, camphene, limonene, linalool, borneol and camphor

What are its therapeutic actions?
Rosemary is
- analgesic
- antiseptic
- antispasmodic
- antiviral
- astringent
- cephalic
- diuretic
- emmenagogue
- hypertensive
- rubefacient
- stimulant
- nervine
- vulnerary
- cordial
- tonic
- uplifting.

Which conditions/systems benefit from its use?
- *skin*: effective astringent, eases puffiness and clears congested dull skin
- *skeletal*: joint problems including arthritis, rheumatism, bursitis
- *muscular*: pain relief for sport/exercise-related injuries/pains
- *circulatory*: rubefacient thus stimulates poor circulation, tonifies heart, improves low blood pressure
- *nervous*: refreshes and clears the mind; improves and aids memory; relieves mental fatigue and lethargy; also activates the brain and stimulates nerve endings (useful for stroke patients); relieves headaches, migraines and vertigo
- *respiratory*: flu, colds, sinusitis, chest infections
- *general*: diuretic thus aids fluid retention and obesity.

When shouldn't it be used?
During pregnancy or for those with epilepsy or high blood pressure.

If you remember only one thing...
Rosemary, like lavender is a good all-round oil, stimulating both mind and body and especially useful for PMT, circulatory problems and infections.

Sandalwood

Sandalwood has been used for medical and therapeutic purposes for over 4000 years.

What is its botanical name?
Santalum album.

Which plant family does it come from?
Santalaceae

Where in the world does it come from?
East India, Sri Lanka and Australia.

Which part of the plant is used to make the oil?
Timber, inner heartwood and roots.

How is it extracted?
Water or steam distillation.

What is its chemical make-up?
Sandalwood is made up of α & β santalol (Alcohol), α & β santalene

What are its therapeutic actions?
Sandalwood is
- antidepressant
- antispasmodic
- antiseptic
- bactericidal
- cicatrisant
- expectorant
- relaxing
- sedative
- tonic.

Which conditions/systems benefit from its use?
- *skin*: soothes dry, irritated, chapped skins; eczema; sensitive skins, calms redness of broken capillaries and reduces high colouring
- *nervous*: soothes tension, relieves stress, insomnia and anxiety
- *respiratory*: throat and chest infections, bronchitis; sedates dry, tickly coughs
- *urinary*: infections, cystitis, cleansing effect on kidneys.

When shouldn't it be used?
Sandalwood has no known contra-indications.

If you remember only one thing…
Sandalwood is widely used in perfumes and is a relaxing and soothing oil, especially good for calming irritations, whether of the nerves, skin or chest. Santalum spicatum is sometimes used in place of Santalum album. It has similar properties but is especially useful for its anti-inflammatory and antiviral effects.

Did you know?

Many male toiletries contain sandalwood.

Tea tree

What is its botanical name?
Melaleuca alternifolia.

Which plant family does it come from?
Myrtaceae

Where in the world does it come from?
Australia.

Which part of the plant is used to make the oil?
The leaves and twigs of the tree.

How is it extracted?
Water or steam distillation.

What is its chemical make-up?
Tea tree may consist of terpinen-4-ol (Alcohol), 1-8 cineole, and pinene

What are its therapeutic actions?
Tea tree is
- anti-inflammatory
- antiseptic
- antiviral
- bactericidal
- cooling
- fungicidal
- immuno-stimulant
- sudorific
- vulnerary
- tonic.

Which conditions/systems benefit from its use?
- *skin*: any fungal or viral infections: cold sores and spots (used neat), acne, athlete's foot, warts, verrucas; infected wounds or boils; blisters, burns, sunburn, dandruff, general itching
- *lymphatic*: glandular fever
- *nervous*: revitalises the mind
- *respiratory*: flu, colds, catarrh, promotes sweating so can reduce fever
- *urinary*: thrush, cystitis, urinary tract infections
- *immune*: boosts the immune system, thus can help shorten time of illness by helping body's defences to fight back
- *general*: useful to prepare body for an operation and to help it recover.

When shouldn't it be used?
Tea tree is generally safe but can irritate the skin in some cases.

If you remember only one thing...
Tea tree is a rarity amongst oils in that it has been proven to have an effect on all three types of infection that attack the body: bacteria, viruses and fungi (see Davis, *Aromatherapy: an A-Z*, p. 295). It is therefore useful both for treating infection and preventing it. It is *the* all-round first-aid oil.

How is it extracted?
By water or steam distillation

What is its chemical make up?
Thyme is made up of Linalool (Alcohol), linalyl acetate, geranyl acetate,

What are its therapeutic actions?
- antiseptic
- antifungal
- antispasmodic
- astringent
- digestive
- expectorant
- emmenagogue
- hypertensive
- mucoylitic
- nervine
- stimulant
- tonic

Which conditions/systems benefit from its use?
- *Skin:* acne, oily skin, boils
- *Muscular:* Arthritis, sports injuries, and rheumatism
- *Circulatory:* Stimulates blood flow , thought to raise blood pressure
- *Nervous:* Headaches, stress, nerve tonic, and mental stimulant
- *Digestive:* Improves appetite, eases flatulence
- *Immune:* Stimulating, tonic for system
- *Respiratory:* coughs, colds, catarrh, bronchitis, flu

When shouldn't it be used?
Thyme is non-toxic and non-irritating, but may cause sensitivity in some people. Use in low dilution. Avoid in pregnancy or cases of hypertension.

If you remember only one thing…
Thyme is a powerful antiseptic useful for stimulating the immune system.

Thyme
What is its botanical name?
Thymus vulgaris

Which plant family does it come from?
Lamiaceae (Labiatae)

Where in the world does it come from?
Mediterranean, Southern Italy

Which part of the plant is used to make the oil?
Fresh or dried leaves and flowers

Vetiver

What is its botanical name?
Vetiveria zizanoides.

Which plant family does it come from?
Poaceae (Gramineae)

Where in the world does it come from?
It is native to South India and Indonesia but is also cultivated throughout the world, in South America, Reunion, Java and Haiti.

Which part of the plant is used to make the oil?
The roots and rootlets which are washed, dried and chopped.

How is it extracted?
By steam distillation.

What is its chemical make-up?
Vetiver may consist of vetiverol (Alcohol), vetivene and vetiverone

What are its therapeutic actions?
Vetiver is
- relaxing
- rubefacient
- sedative
- stimulant
- vermifuge
- nervine
- tonic.

Which conditions/systems benefit from its use?
- *skin*: helps heal acne scars
- *muscular*: eases aches and pains
- *circulatory*: increases blood flow, mild rubefacient.
- *nervous*: the mind benefits the most from vetiver; it calms the central nervous system, reduces tension, worry, anxiety and any stress-related symptoms; relieves insomnia and nervous debility
- *reproductive*: tonic.

When shouldn't it be used?
Vetiver has no known contraindications.

If you remember only one thing...
Vetiver is the oil of tranquillity. It has a tranquillising, grounding effect, bringing the user back down to earth, helping relaxation and the release of mental and physical exhaustion.

Ylang ylang

Which plant family does it come from?
Annonaceae

What is its botanical name?
Cananga odorata.

Where in the world does it come from?
Indonesia, the Philippines, Madagascar.

Which part of the plant is used to make the oil?
Flower petals.

How is it extracted?
By steam distillation.

What is its chemical make-up?
Ylang ylang may consist of β-caryophyllene (Sesquiterpene), -farnesene, methyl benzoate, benzyl acetate, linalool, geraniol, and pinene

What are its therapeutic actions?
Ylang ylang is
- antidepressant
- aphrodisiac
- hypotensive
- relaxing
- sedative
- tonic.

Which conditions/systems benefit from its use?
- *skin*: balances sebum production both for oily and dry skins; extractive effect on acne i.e. draws out the spot and infection (so it will get worse before getting better)
- *circulatory*: slows over-rapid breathing (hyperpnea) and heartbeat (tachycardia); reduces high blood pressure
- *nervous*: antidepressant, creates feelings of joy, calms central nervous system
- *endocrine*: regulates flow of adrenaline and thus slows its effects reducing stress, anger, frustration, panic, fear and shock; balances hormones
- *reproductive*: tonic for womb; impotence, frigidity.

When shouldn't it be used?
Ylang ylang has a very heady perfume and can cause headaches and nausea. It should therefore be used in moderation.

If you remember only one thing...
Ylang ylang has a euphoric effect, promoting positive emotions in the user and is calming and sedating in times of stress.

DON'T FORGET TO USE YOUR RESOURCE CD ROM

- TEST YOUR KNOWLEDGE OF ESSENTIAL OILS

- TEST YOUR KNOWLEDGE QUESTIONS

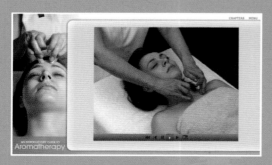

- FULL VIDEO OF PRACTICAL SKILLS

AND MUCH MORE!

An introductory guide to Aromatherapy

7 How to use essential oils at home

Putting drops of essential oil into a burner.

In Brief

This chapter explains the different and most effective methods of using essential oils at home.

Essential oils are very easy to use at home for medical and non-medical purposes. Many common ailments can be treated by using oils in the bath, in creams and lotions and in steam inhalations.

NB a medical professional and/or professional aromatherapist should be consulted for serious medical and psychological conditions.

Massage

Massage is the most common application method. The warmth of the hands helps to move the oil across the skin and work it into the affected area. The essential oil should be blended with the chosen carrier oil (see Chapter 5 for more detailed information on blending and carrier oils) in the following dilutions:

1. 2 drops to 5ml (one teaspoon) for adults
2. 6 drops to 15ml (three teaspoons or one tablespoon)
3. 20 drops to 50ml (10 teaspoons).

Once blended, essential oils will share the shelf life of the carrier oil they are mixed with so it is best not to mix more than is needed. The following suggested amounts will obviously need to be adapted for smaller/larger frames, children and the elderly:

1. a face massage requires 5ml carrier oil
2. a full body massage requires 20-25ml carrier oil
3. a specific area of the body (e.g. hands, feet, arm, neck) may require from 5-15ml oil.

Compresses

A compress is a piece of material that has been soaked in water and is then placed over an affected part of the body and held in place for a period of time. Both hot and cold compresses can be used: hot compresses are more useful for muscular aches and pains, earaches and toothaches whereas cold compresses are better for joint sprains and headaches. Essential oil is mixed with the water before adding the material. To make a compress:

1. fill a bowl with 100mls of hot or cold water and add one drop of the chosen essential oil
2. soak a piece of material (e.g. a flannel or unmedicated gauze) in the bowl of water
3. squeeze out the excess water and place the material over the affected area
4. cover with cling film to hold the material in place and leave for approximately two hours
5. the compress will soon cool down/warm up. Repeat the process as long as is necessary/desired.

Baths

Probably the easiest and most everyday way to use essential oils is to put them in the bath. Remember, though, that essential oils do not dissolve in water and will only float or sink. Therefore they

A foot bath.

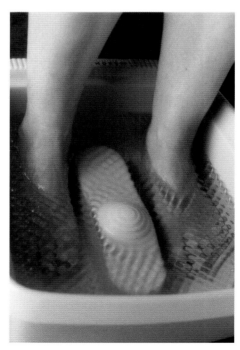

should be mixed with a small quantity of an emulsifier, preferably unperfumed, such as shampoo, liquid soap, shower gel, or even full cream milk before adding them to the bath. Skin irritants (e.g. spicy oils such as black pepper) are not recommended for a relaxing bath! To use oils in the bath:

- run a hot, but not over-hot, bath
- close the doors and windows (this seals the aromatic scent in the room for maximum benefit)
- mix up to six drops of essential oil in a carrier oil, or emulsifier
- add the mixture to the water agitate then soak and enjoy!

Baths can also be used for a particular part of the body. For a foot/hand bath mix two drops of essential oil in a bowl of warm water and soak the affected foot/hand for about 20 minutes. For haemorrhoids, childbirth stitches and genital infections like thrush, sitting in a warm bath (known as a sitz bath) containing two or three drops of essential oil can help. Again the oils should be mixed with an emulsifier. Tea tree is good for thrush and lavender oil helps healing after childbirth.

Vaporisers

Essential oils can be vaporised (warmed so that they evaporate and spread their aroma around a room) either in an oil burner, on a light bulb ring or using the heat of a radiator. Electric diffusers may also be used.

- **Burner**: burners are usually a small bowl placed over a nightlight candle. The heat from the candle evaporates whatever is in the bowl. It is best to use a glazed, non-porous burner. Put water in the small bowl, add two drops of the chosen essential oil to the water and light the candle. The bowl should not be allowed to burn dry because this causes a bitter smell.

Burners can be used for general atmosphere (e.g. to relax, uplift, soothe) or for more specific purposes such as keeping insects away (lemongrass is a good insect repellent).

- **Diffusers**: These have an electric pump and emit a fine mist of oil/essence. Manufacturers instructions on operation and the use of oils should be followed.
- **Light bulbs**: the heat from a light bulb can be used to evaporate essential oils. About two drops of oil is usually enough for each use. Light bulb rings and attachments should be fitted when the light is off and the bulb is cool.
- **Radiators**: place two drops of essential oil onto a cotton wool ball and place it on, or behind a radiator when it is on. The heat from the radiator will evaporate the oil.

Putting drops of essential oil onto a light bulb ring.

Inhalation

Essential oils can be added to very hot water and then inhaled in the steam. This is very effective for respiratory problems and sinus infections, clearing the mucus and blocked noses associated with colds and flu. It is also good for brightening the complexion and clearing the skin of blocked pores and excess oil. Steam inhalation is not recommended for asthmatics.

1. fill a bowl, or a sink, with hot water
2. add two drops of the chosen essential oil (eucalyptus and peppermint are good for respiratory infections; tea tree helps the skin)
3. lean over the bowl, not too close to the water, and cover your head with a cloth or towel so that the bowl is enclosed by the material (which helps keep the oil's valuable aroma close to the affected area)
4. keeping eyes closed, inhale the steam for several minutes.

Creams, gels, lotions and face masks

Many commercially-produced face creams, masks and body lotions contain essential oils but it is easy and cheaper to make your own. Any unperfumed cream gel or lotion can be mixed with a few drops of essential oil to make an individually perfumed product. It is best to use a home-made cream or one which clearly states its contents, since some may contain chemicals that react with the essential oil, or counteract its therapeutic effects. Some of the most suitable creams are sold by suppliers of essential oils. Follow the dilutions used for massage oils (i.e. two drops of essential oil per 5ml teaspoon of cream/lotion). A basic face mask, either home-made or commercial, can be customised with a drop of essential oil. Powder clays may be purchased from suppliers, which can then be mixed with essences or hydrosols to treat skin conditions. Select the oils and clays suitable for the clients skin type; for example pink clay and Roman chamomile (hydrosol or essence) for sensitive skin, green clay and cedarwood (hydrosol or essence) for congested skin. If using essences, add one drop to approximately one tablespoon of the clay, using warm water to blend into a workable consistency. If using a hydrosol, mix with the clay to a smooth consistency. Apply with a brush, leave to dry for approximately 10 minutes. Remove with warm water and sponges. If applying on the face, avoid the eye area. To prevent skin reactions, oils known to cause irritation should be avoided.

Flower waters/ hydrolats/ hydrosols

Steam distillation of a plant to extract the essential oil produces an oily water (see Chapter 2 for more details). The essential oil floats to the top and is separated off, leaving water which will be scented by traces of the oil (for example distillation of lavender will produce lavender oil and lavender water). This is a hydrolat, flower water or hydrosol. Hydrolats contain minute quantities of essential oils and water. They are safe to use neat without further dilution unless labelled otherwise. Hydrolats have similar therapeutic qualities to the oil they derive from, even though they do not have exactly the same chemical make-up: thus just as lavender oil is

versatile so is lavender water. They have been used for centuries in skin preparations and perfumes. Flower waters can be used for cosmetic purposes (rose water and orange-flower water are both sold as skin tonics) or for the treatment of skin conditions, especially those like eczema which would be aggravated by using a cream these can be applied to the skin using a spray. They can also be used around the house, e.g. in baths or for scenting pot pourri. In the Mediterranean and North Africa, orange-flower water is used in cooking, for scenting cakes and dishes such as couscous. They are very gentle and safe and thus provide a useful introduction to essential oils.

Shampoos

If you have fair hair you may have used a chamomile shampoo in the past, whereas if you have dark hair you may have used a rosemary shampoo (both are said to enhance the different colours). Make your own by mixing two drops of the chosen essential oil with an unperfumed, mild shampoo. Citrus oils will have a refreshing effect on mind and body as will peppermint; flower oils can be used as perfume and soothing oils (like frankincense) will help relaxation.

Neat

Neat application of essential oils, without blending them first or adding them to water, is not recommended. However there are two exceptions. Tea tree can be used neat on spots and lavender oil can be used on wounds and burns.

You now know all the methods of using essential oils at home for common ailments and general well-being. For more serious conditions and problems, a professional aromatherapist should always be consulted.

DON'T FORGET TO
USE YOUR RESOURCE
CD ROM

- TEST YOUR KNOWLEDGE OF ESSENTIAL OILS

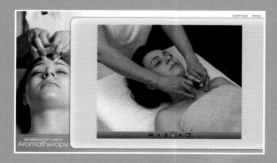

- TEST YOUR KNOWLEDGE QUESTIONS

- FULL VIDEO OF PRACTICAL SKILLS

AND MUCH MORE!

An introductory guide to Aromatherapy

8 Aromatherapy massage

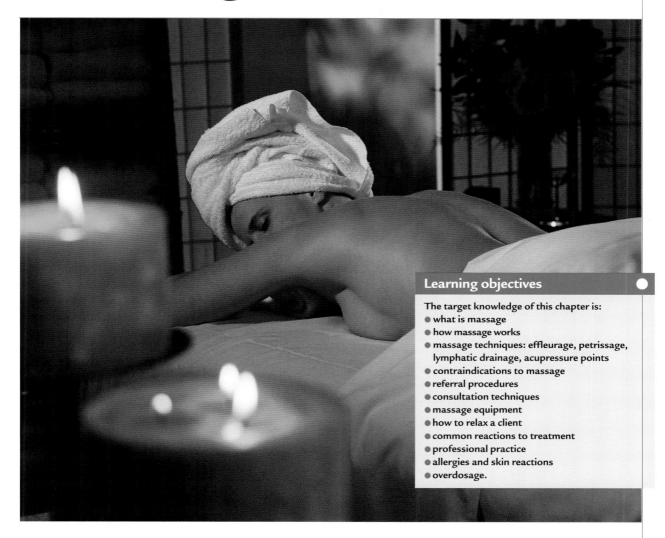

Learning objectives

The target knowledge of this chapter is:
- what is massage
- how massage works
- massage techniques: effleurage, petrissage, lymphatic drainage, acupressure points
- contraindications to massage
- referral procedures
- consultation techniques
- massage equipment
- how to relax a client
- common reactions to treatment
- professional practice
- allergies and skin reactions
- overdosage.

In Brief

This chapter focuses on one particular method of using essential oils, massage. Professionally, this is the most common method of application because the skin absorbs essential oils very easily and effectively. The next chapter explains different massage techniques and how to use them on different parts of the body, as well as explaining certain complementary massage therapies such as acupressure and lymphatic drainage.

WHAT IS MASSAGE?

Massage is the use of the hands to manipulate the soft tissues of the body thus relaxing either a specific area or the whole person. In a way, it is an extension of the basic rub that we give either ourselves, a friend, or a child when we or they bang or knock themselves unexpectedly. Touch is both physically and mentally soothing. It

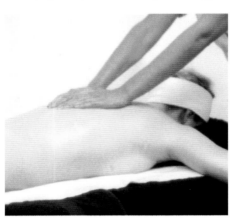

can also be stimulating: think of rubbing the eyes or the face when tired to wake ourselves up, or rubbing an arm or leg that has 'gone to sleep'. All of these actions are forms of massage.

What is aromatherapy massage?

Aromatherapy massage is concerned with relaxing clients and helping them, through the physical and aromatic effects of essential oils, with certain physical and emotional conditions. Using a blend of carrier and essential oils in the correct dilutions, the aromatherapist massages the affected area or the whole body depending on the symptoms and treatment.

You now know what aromatherapy massage is. The next section explains how it works and the different techniques involved.

HOW DOES AROMATHERAPY MASSAGE WORK?

The heat of the hands helps the absorption of the oil by the skin. Different massage techniques encourage relaxation, better circulation, improved suppleness and/or the release of muscular tension.

What are these techniques?

In aromatherapy massage there are two main techniques used: effleurage and petrissage. Both derive from French: effleurer means to touch lightly or to brush against whereas petrissage means to knead or rub with force, like a baker kneading dough. Thus effleurage is a light, soothing stroke whereas petrissage is a more forceful, thorough kneading movement. Lymphatic drainage massage and acupressure are also recommended.

● **Effleurage**

An effleurage stroke is smooth, gentle and flowing. Pressure is applied slowly, without jerks or breaks, towards the heart (i.e. from the waist towards the shoulders or from the foot towards the thigh). The rhythmic movement helps to relax the client and encourage the release of tension. Effleurage is usually the stroke used to start and finish a massage on a particular limb or area. It can be used in up and down movements or circles. It is a relaxing stroke.

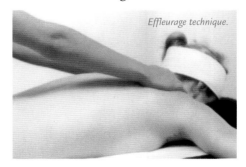

Effleurage technique.

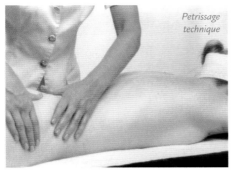
Petrissage technique

Pressure point technique

● Petrissage

Petrissage is a compression movement and it is therefore only possible on areas of the body where there is enough tissue to compress.

● Vibrations

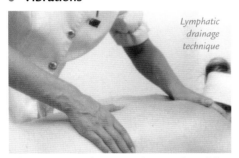
Lymphatic drainage technique

Vibrations can be carried out using either one or both hands and either whole palms or just the fingertips. Using contractions within their own muscles, the aromatherapist creates tremors, which pass into the muscles of the client, releasing pain and tension. These can be stimulating or soothing.

● Passive joint movements

Passive movements require the client to relax and let the aromatherapist gently take a joint (e.g., knee, elbow, shoulder) through its natural range of movement. These movements may help to improve mobility and release tension.

● Lymphatic drainage massage

The lymphatic system is a secondary circulation that aids the removal of waste. It collects toxins and excess fluid from cells and tissues, filters off bacteria, produces antibodies and returns the filtered fluid and antibodies to the blood. Some massage techniques can help the action of the lymphatic system, aiding the removal of toxins and boosting the immune system. It is useful for treating fluid retention or oedema (swelling). Lymphatic drainage massage consists of:

- soft, pumping movements pushing in the direction of the lymph nodes
- light pressure: the lymph vessels are near the surface of the skin so pressure should be gentle not firm.

● Pressure point techniques

Acupressure is a variation of acupuncture, a Chinese therapy. Whereas acupuncture involves inserting very fine needles into certain points in the skin in order to help energy, known as chi, flow more smoothly through the body, acupressure uses finger or thumb pressure on the same points. It can be used during aromatherapy massage in the form of pressure point techniques to help treat various conditions (see Chapter 10: Other complementary therapies).

Why are continuous movements necessary?

One hand or both should always be kept on the body being massaged during the treatment since as soon as the hands are removed the body will register this as the end of the massage and begin to 'change gear', and the client will think about getting ready to dress and leave.

THE ROUTINE

This is a suggested aromatherapy massage routine. It should be performed extremely slowly and could take up to 1 and half to 2 hours to perform fully as the emphasis is on relaxation, lymphatic drainage and pressure points to aid the absorption of the oils.

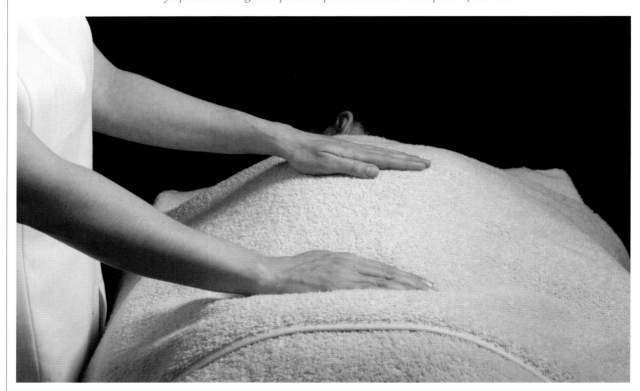

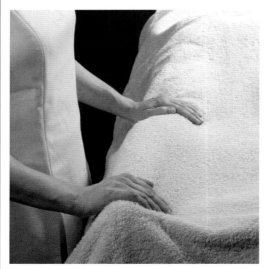
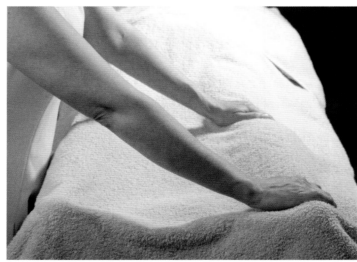

Begin with y your hands placed over the towels on the clinets head and lower back area. Slowly move to the hip and ankle giving the client a reassuring press through the towels to help them relax and get used to your touch

AROMATHERAPY

Back of the leg

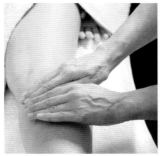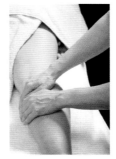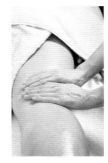

Laying on of hands

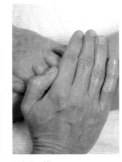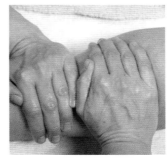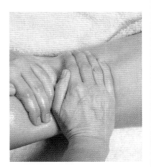

6 full effleurage

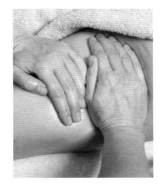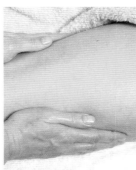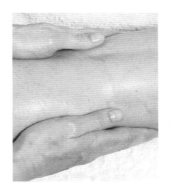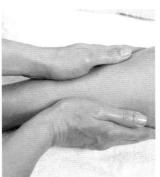

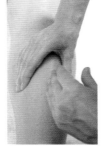

picking up on the Achilles tendon   *Picking up on the gastrocnemius*   *Splitting of the gastrocnemius*

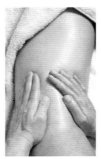
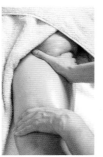

Push and pull on the whole leg · *6 sets of Palmar kneading to the thigh* · *v shaped lymphatic drainage on the thigh*

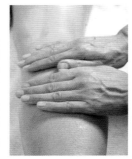

6 full effleurage · *laying on of hands*

Back massage

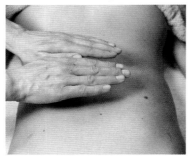
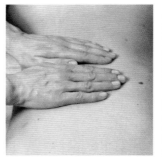
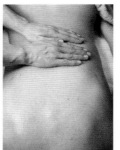
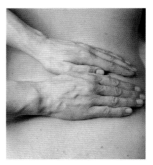

Laying on of hands

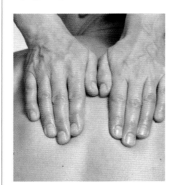
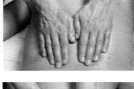

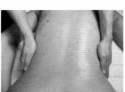
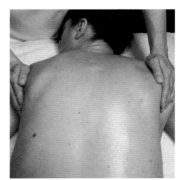

12 reverse effleurage

 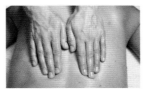 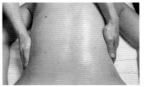 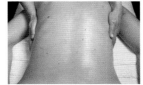

3 sets of effleurage around the systems — respiratory, digestive, urinary

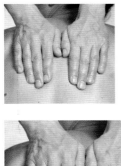 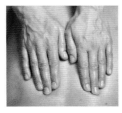 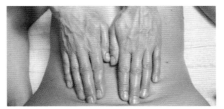 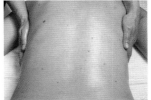

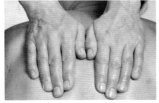   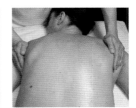

2 sets of pressure points from the sacrum to the crown which can be performed with either the thumbs or re-inforced fingers.
(Pressure points should be held for a count of 2 seconds pressure — hold for 2 counts — release, slide to the next point and repeat)

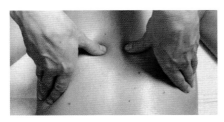 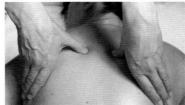 

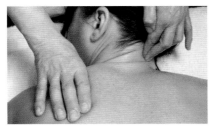  

CASE STUDIES

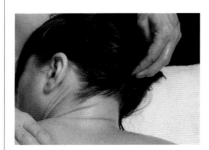
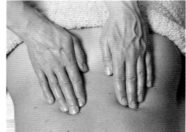
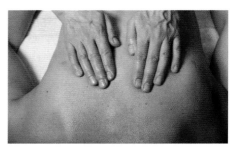

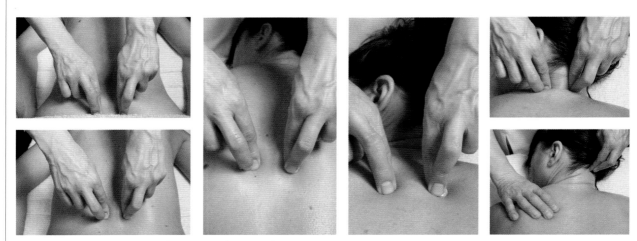

2 sets of rotational pressures from the sacrum to the occipital

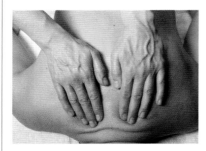
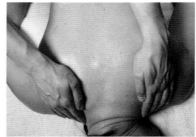
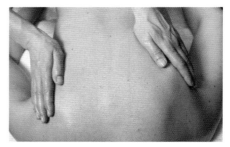

Move to the side of the couch and perform 12 effleurage stokes from the sacrum to the occipital and return

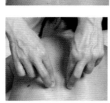
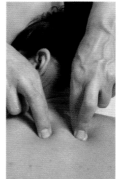
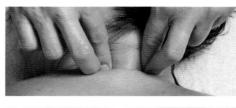

2 sets of rotational pressures from the sacrum to the occipital

AROMATHERAPY

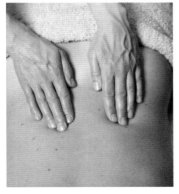 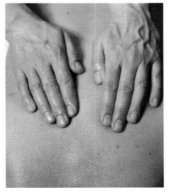 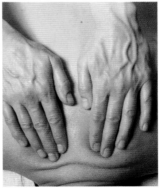 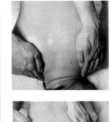

Move to the side of the couch and perform 12 effleurage stokes from the sacrum to the occipital and return

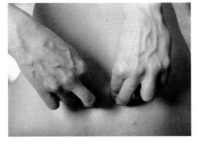 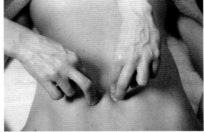 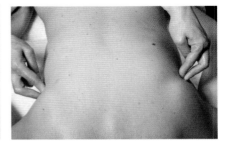

Pressure points around the shoulder girdle

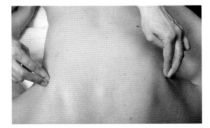  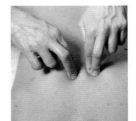 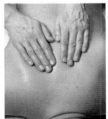

Rotational pressure points around the shoulder girdle as above

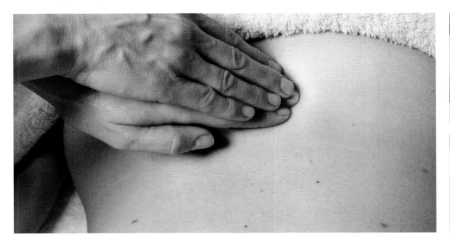 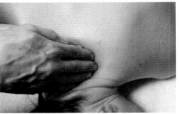 

Reinforced pressure points either side of the spine

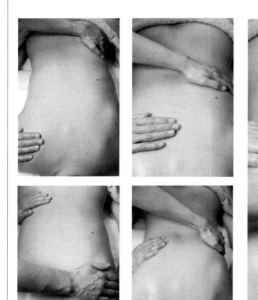

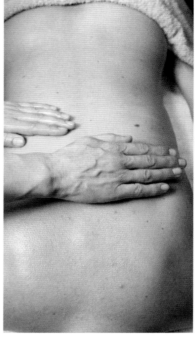

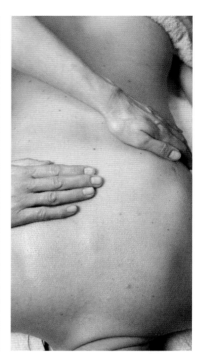

Push and pull lymphatic drainage to the whole back *Alternate stroking across the whole back*

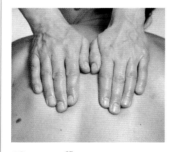

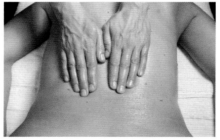

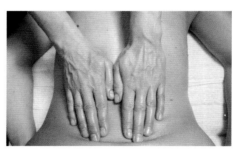

12 reverse effleurage

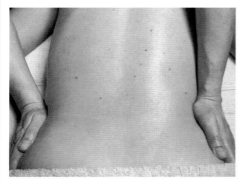

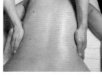

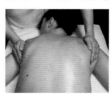

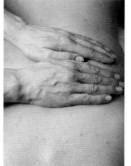

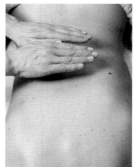

laying on of hands

AROMATHERAPY

Facial massage

  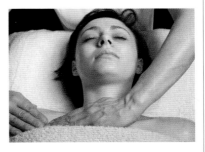

Laying on of hands on the chest

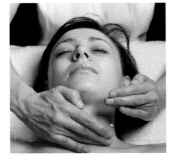 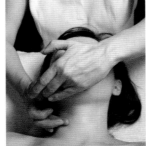  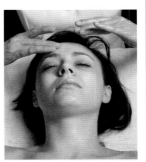

effleurage the whole face using alternate stoking with the ring finger

 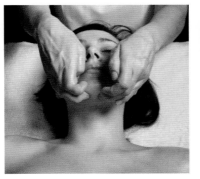 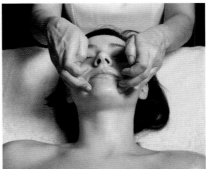

Pressure points clavicle to crown

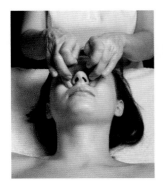 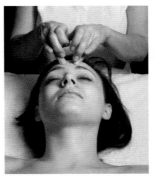 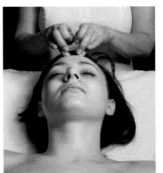 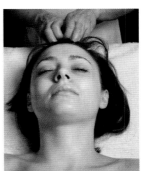

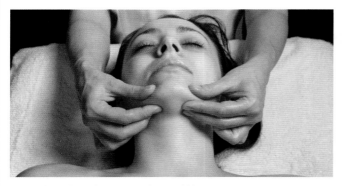

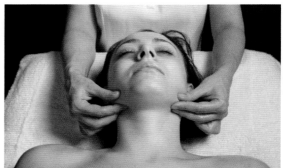

6 sets of lymphatic drainage on the mandible

  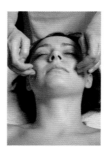  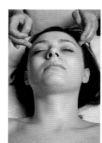 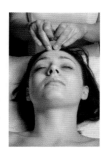

Pressure points from the clavicle to the zygomatic bone and across to the pre-auricular lymph nodes. Continue Pressure points around the perimeter of the face (hair line) onto the forehead

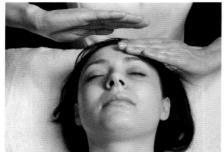  

20 sets of Alternate stroking on the forehead

6 sets of eye circles

AROMATHERAPY

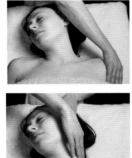
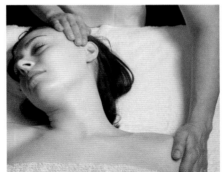
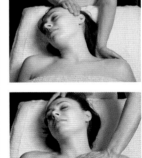

return to the chest using the ring finger only to continue with 6 sets of stoking up either side of the neck

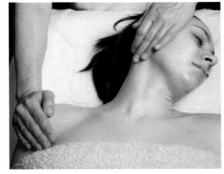

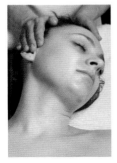
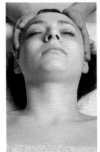
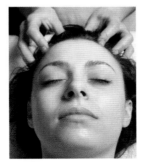
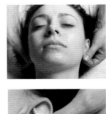

kneading to the scalp   kneading on the ears   Pulling through the hair

3 full effleurage including scalp and hair

CASE STUDIES

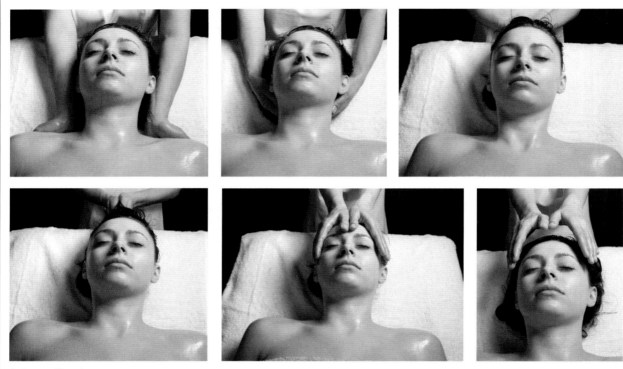

laying on of hands

Arms

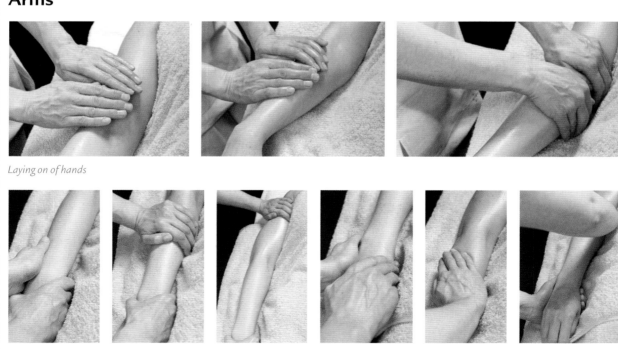

Laying on of hands

6 full effleurage

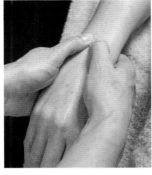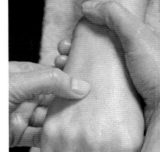

6 sets of kneading around the carpal bones

2 sets of kneading between the metacarpals

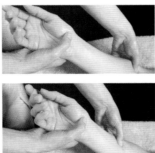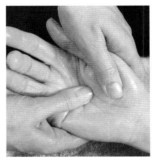

kneading of the phalangeal joints with finger pulls

6 sets of kneading on the thenar and hyper thenar eminence

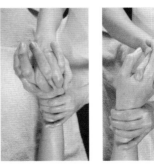

2 sets of kneading up to the supra-trochlear lymph nodes

3 sets of wrist rotations clockwise and anti clockwise

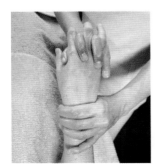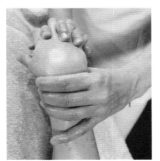

3 sets of flexion and extension to the wrist

Laying on of hands

CASE STUDIES

Abdominal massage

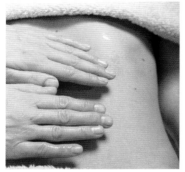 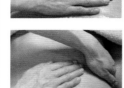   

Laying on of hands
6 sets of circular effleurage

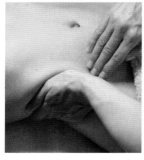  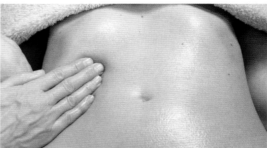  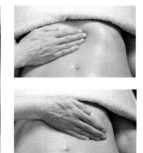 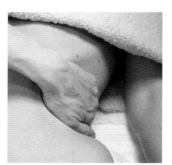

6 breathing movements

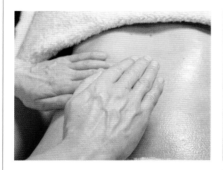

6 sets of pulling either side of the obliques

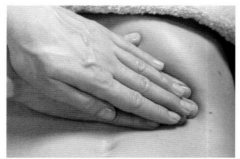 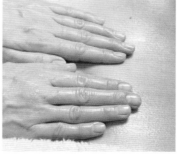 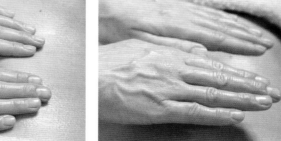

Massage to the solar plexus, 6 full effleurage as before *laying on of hands*

Front of leg massage

  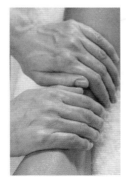  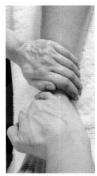

Laying on of hands   *6 full effleurage*

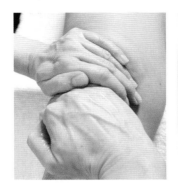 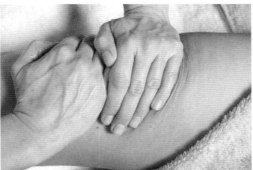 

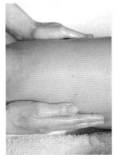   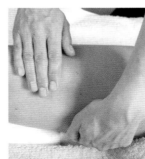 

push and pull lymphatic drainage on the thigh

  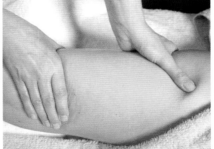 

12 sets of V shaped lymphatic drainage on the thigh

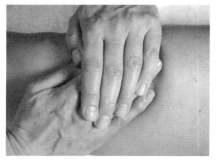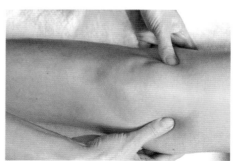

6 sets of effleurage up to and around the patella

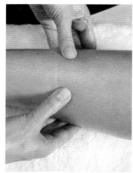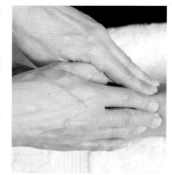

1 set of kneading down the tibia

6 sets of stroking around the tarsals

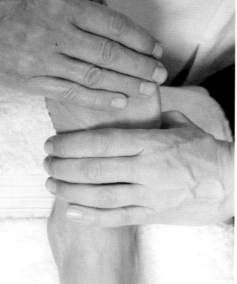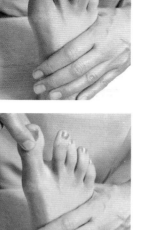

1 set of kneading between the metatarsals

1 set of full toe rotations

1 set of individual toe rotations

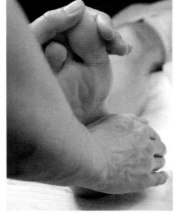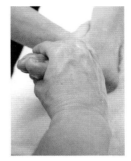

6 sets of stroking to the sole   *3 sets of flexion and extension of the ankle*

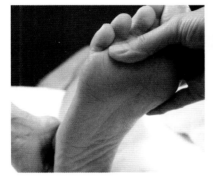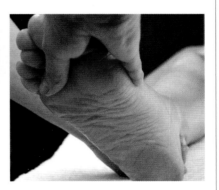

rotate the ankle clockwise and anti — clockwise

6 full sets of effleurage

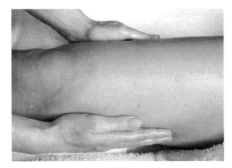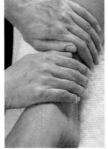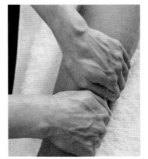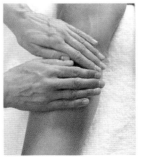

laying on of hands

Finishing sequence

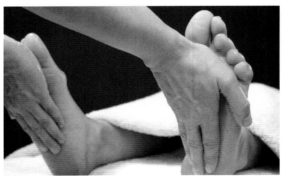
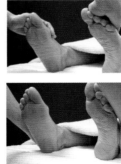
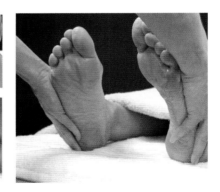

Laying on of hands to the soles of the feet

6 effleurage of the feet

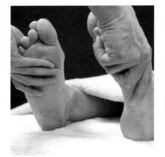

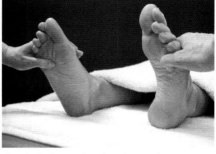

Place your hands flat against the soles of the feet and hold for 5 seconds

thumb circling on the solar plexus point – approx 10 seconds

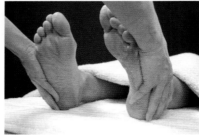

3 sets of effleurage to the feet extending the ankles, and repeat

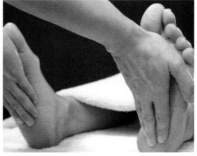

Hold the feet as in point

Slowly take your hands away whilst one hand covers the feet with towels

When is aromatherapy massage not recommended?

Although aromatherapy massage is generally safe it may be contraindicated at times.

With medical, GP or specialist permission – In circumstances where written medical permission cannot be obtained, clients must sign an informed consent form stating that the treatment and its effects have been explained to them and confirm that they are willing to proceed without permission from their GP.

· Pregnancy (use only mandarin)
· Cardiovascular conditions (thrombosis, phlebitis, hypertension, hypotension, heart conditions) · Haemophilia · Any condition already being treated by a GP or another complementary practitioner · Medical oedema · Osteoporosis · Arthritis · Nervous/ Psychotic conditions · Epilepsy · Recent operations · Diabetes · Asthma · Any dysfunction of the nervous system (e.g. Multiple Sclerosis, Parkinson's disease, Motor Neurone disease) · Bell's Palsy · Trapped/Pinched nerve (e.g. sciatica) · Inflamed nerve · Cancer · Spastic conditions · Kidney infections · Hormonal implants · Undiagnosed pain · When taking prescribed medication · Acute rheumatism · Cervical spondylitis · Whiplash · Slipped disc

Contraindications that restrict treatment

· Fever · Contagious or infectious diseases · Under the influence of alcohol or recreational drugs · Diarrhoea and vomiting · Skin diseases · Undiagnosed lumps and bumps · Localised swelling · Inflammation · Menstration (abdomen – first few days) · Varicose veins · Pregnancy (abdomen) · Breast feeding · Cuts · Bruises · Abrasions · Scar tissues (2 years for major operation and 6 months for a small scar) · Sunburn · Haematoma · Recent fractures (minimum 3 months) · Gastric ulcers · Hernia · After a heavy meal · Hypersensitive skin

NB All known allergies should be checked

Client contraindications should be checked against the safety data for each oil prior to treatment

Referral procedures

There will be occasions when you are unsure whether to proceed with a treatment. It is not the job of the aromatherapist to diagnose medical problems or decide if a condition is treatable – in fact the code of conduct of many professional associations, such as the CThA, states that diagnosis is not allowed.

You now know how to use massage and when not to use it. The next section describes the different practicalities required in giving an aromatherapy massage.

CONSULTATION TECHNIQUES

NB For the purpose of this section the person receiving the treatment will be known as the client.

Consultation techniques

Before beginning an aromatherapy massage, or a series of treatments, the aromatherapist will need to talk to the client in order to find out why they have

come for a treatment e.g. is it for a physical condition (e.g. muscular aches and pains), for a psychological problem (e.g. anxiety, depression) or simply for relaxation? In order to discuss this, clients will need to feel relaxed and, since relaxation is also an important part of the whole treatment, the consultation can be a useful way to help both aromatherapist and client to feel comfortable with each other. It also gives the aromatherapist a chance to:

- find out what the client expects
- Assess client suitability for treatment
- explain the treatment and the possible effects (i.e. dispelling any unrealistic or even cynical expectations)
- Discuss possible contra-actions
- find out if there are any contraindications
- Patch test any oils if necessary
- Recommend the most suitable method of treatment
- select oils that will suit the client and the treatment
- fill out the consultation forms
- agree the treatment plan with the client.
- chose and recommend suitable essences, fixed oils and other media and methods of use. Details should be included on plant families, common and botanical names of essences, treatment media used, blending ratios and treatment methods
- ask the client (or appointed advocate) to sign to endorse any recommended blends
- ask the client (or appointed advocate) to sign to consent to the treatment
- refer client to another practitioner if necessary

The following topics should be covered by a consultation:

- personal details: name, address, telephone number, date of birth, GP's name and address
- medical background: medicines being taken (prescription and non-prescription medicines including homeopathic ones); medical conditions (any contraindications or

problems should be referred; whatever the background a disclaimer form should be sent to the GP for confirmation that aromatherapy will not have any adverse effects); previous illnesses or hereditary diseases; operations; allergies.

- diet and other factors: eating habits, fluid and alcohol consumption, smoker or non-smoker, sleep problems (like insomnia).
- client preferences in terms of odour/scents
- Reason for treatment

How to carry out a consultation

First, you need a space to consult in. A private, comfortable area, where there will be no interruptions would be suitable. Try to arrange the room/space in an open, inviting way and ensure that your own body language is positive and open e.g. sitting with arms and legs crossed facing away from the client is a very closed and unfriendly stance. Also, sitting behind a desk or standing whilst the client sits may be perceived as threatening. Try to sit facing the client, at the same height, not behind a table or desk. The client must feel relaxed enough to explain the problem/reason that has made them come for an aromatherapy massage. This is where the aromatherapist needs to demonstrate listening and encouraging skills.

How to find out what you need to know

Many clients consulting with an aromatherapist for the first time may be nervous and unwilling to reveal much information about why they have come, either through embarrassment, anxiety or shyness. An open and relaxed person will usually volunteer the required information but with more reticent clients the aromatherapist needs to know how to ask a question as well as how to listen to the answers.

- Start with general questions or, if you want a prompt or sense a particularly shy client, use the form/record card as a starting point. Once you have begun asking questions which are easy to answer (name, address, date of birth etc) the more difficult ones about treatment and contraindications won't seem so daunting – the client will be in the rhythm of responding to your questions and will expect them rather than be made more nervous by them.

- Ask open not closed questions: ones that cannot be answered with yes or no. For example, ask what do you expect from an aromatherapy massage rather than do you expect the massage to work or tell me about your diet rather than do you eat healthily? No one likes to examine their own habits so it is best to address the questions in as open and unthreatening a manner as possible.

- In order to instil trust, use your own body language to encourage and aid responses: nodding, smiling and leaning forward all communicate interest as does keeping eye contact. Looking away frequently, fidgeting or staring blankly will merely communicate nervousness and/or lack of interest which will not help the client to feel confident in your abilities or your interest in them. Remember that, as an aromatherapist, you are there to help the client: if you are unfriendly, nervous or uncommunicative the client is likely to pick up on this and react in a similar way.

- Be confident, enthusiastic and professional.

- Communicate your own belief and trust in the treatment: this will help the client to believe in it and will improve the psychological and physiological effects of the massage.

- Reassure the client that everything discussed will remain completely confidential and make sure that you never break this confidence.

- Treat everyone equally: if you cannot avoid bringing racist or sexist prejudices to the massage table aromatherapy is not the profession for you.

- Discuss the possible essential oils with the client as fully as is necessary (i.e. describing the effects and qualities of the oils, not the chemistry!). The client should smell a number of potentially suitable oils before you make the final selection. The aroma of the oils, absorbed via the olfactory tract, is vital to the effectiveness of the treatment. Also if there are any selected oils which are unsuitable (due to association or because the client doesn't like the smell) this can be sorted out before the massage begins. For example, it is no good using a blend with geranium on the client if the smell makes him/her feel sick because the oils will not produce the appropriate therapeutic effect.

- Potential reactions and contra-actions to the treatment should also be discussed in a manner that will not alarm the client. Advise them that they may suffer an increase in symptoms currently experienced, for example, headaches, fatigue, muscular aches or skin reactions. An increase in bowel movements or in the frequency of micturition may also be experienced during the treatment programme. It is important to explain that these reactions are normal and will quickly pass, usually with 24-48 hours. It is useful to balance discussion of contra-actions with details on the benefits of the treatment; after all, you want to encourage the client to have aromatherapy, not put them off completely!

- It is important to find out if the client is taking any medication – prescription or non-prescription (such as homeopathy) as the essences may interact adversely or counteract the medication in some way.

- Discussion with the client during the consultation will enable you to determine their needs in respect of their health and well being. By ascertaining the client's expectations, you will be able to plan a suitable treatment programme incorporating the most beneficial oils, carriers and treatment methods.

- After carefully selecting the essences and massage media with full client cooperation, it is essential to obtain a signature of endorsement. Ask the client to sign to confirm acceptance of the blend(s) chosen. These should be fully documented on the consultation form, and include details of the choice of essences, fixed oils and other media, blending ratios and justification for the blend(s). Methods of use should also be noted. In circumstance, such as in a care environment, where the clients are unable to sign themselves, a legally appointed companion or advocate should sign to accept the blends chosen and to consent to the treatment on their behalf.

You now know how to find out the necessary information required to give an effective and safe treatment. The next section explains the equipment that is needed and other practical considerations.

WHERE TO GIVE AN AROMATHERAPY MASSAGE

Aromatherapy massage requires the person receiving the massage to be partly or completely undressed (underwear should be kept on). The room where the massage takes place should therefore be private and without risk of interruption. Fear of interruption will usually counteract all the positive, relaxing benefits of the massage. It should also be the correct temperature i.e. not too cold or too warm. You will be much warmer than the client because you will be exerting yourself physically. Make sure that there is a suitable ambient temperature. Towels and blankets or heated blankets can help with both these issues. Towels should be placed under and over the client, covering up any area of the body which is not currently being massaged. A blanket may be used on top of the towel at the beginning of the massage or during it, as necessary, to keep the client warm.

What equipment is needed?

- **a massage couch**

In order to comfortably and effectively perform a massage a proper adjustable massage couch is recommended covered with possibly a blanket and then towels. Remember that whoever gives the massage should be comfortable and not adopting bad postures that may cause back or neck ache. A couch that can be adjusted to the right height for each individual prevents such problems.

- **pillows and towels for support and protection**

Pillows will help both client and aromatherapist. For massage of the back, a pillow or face ring under the face/shoulders and another pillow or supports under the ankles will help improve comfort. Of course, it is best to check with each individual what suits them. For a front of the body massage a pillow under the neck and under the knees will stop them from being unnecessarily stretched and strained during the massage. As mentioned earlier, towels are required to cover the parts of the client which are not being massaged.

- **changing facilities and bathroom**
In a professional situation the client should be able to change and dress in privacy so adequate changing facilities will be required. Also, it is advisable that both the aromatherapist and client go to the toilet before the massage begins to prevent interruption.

- **Essences, fixed oils and other materials**
It is essential to have plentiful supplies of essences, fixed oils, other media and the necessary equipment for blending readily available. The equipment should be positioned to allow for safe and hygienic blending. These items must be securely stored when not in use, to prevent inappropriate access, spillages or degradation of the oils.

A couch set up for massage.

What about the aromatherapist?
The person giving the treatment should be dressed comfortably in professional clothes and comfortable shoes. Nails should be kept short, clean and unvarnished and jewellery avoided. Where necessary, hair should be pinned or tied away from the face and collar. The aromatherapist should not wear perfume as this may interfere with the treatment effects

You now know how to set up an area for giving an aromatherapy treatment and what equipment is required. The next section explains more intangible considerations: relaxation techniques and good professional

RELAXATION TECHNIQUES AND GOOD PRACTICE

practice.
In order for the client to feel relaxed, certain aspects need to be considered. As discussed earlier, the room should be a comfortable temperature, the client's privacy should never be compromised and the aromatherapist should be dressed professionally and tidily. Lighting should be bright enough for the massage to be carried out but not harsh: fluorescent and neon lights can often be over-bright. When settling the client on the couch, check that they are comfortable. Some clients may wish to listen to music or talk, some may prefer silence. Remember that

this is their time and you should respect their wishes – they are not paying to hear your views or personal preferences.

Good professional practice
It is extremely important for any aromatherapist to take the following information into consideration when performing a massage.

- **emotions and sex**
When carrying out an aromatherapy massage it is evident that the client will be semi-naked. His or her modesty is of paramount importance and a

professional aromatherapist will not allow any emotional or sexual involvement with the client to compromise the client's position. Vice-versa, if you feel that the client is behaving inappropriately towards you, you would be perfectly within your rights to discontinue the treatment.

- ### psychology

It is important not to become the client's counsellor. Obviously, if a client feels relaxed and comfortable with the aromatherapist, s/he may talk of their problems/thoughts but the aroma-therapist must resist the temptation to get personally involved, offering judgements or advice. It is also wise to avoid topics of conversation that may cause offence or strong feelings such as money, marriage, religion or politics (especially controversial issues like abortion, capital punishment, immigration).

- ### hygiene

The aromatherapist's equipment (couch, towels, changing room, trolley,

consultation room, blending equipment) should be kept clean at all times and the aromatherapist should also pay attention to his/her personal hygiene since they will be spending intensive periods of time in a confined space with the client. Encourage the client to shower prior to treatment if possible; some establishments have shower facilities available. If there are none, ensure that the client's hands and feet are suitably cleansed prior to commencing the treatment, and remove any make up from their skin if necessary.

Performing an aromatherapy massage

Each massage, just like each aromatherapist and client is individual and it would thus be impossible to provide a perfect massage sequence that suits every practitioner and client. By practising the techniques described above in a suitable environment, an aromatherapist will develop their own routines adapted to each client's needs.

You now know about the practicalities and good practice that should be considered before giving an aromatherapy massage as well as the techniques to use in a routine. The final section explains possible allergic or adverse reactions which a practising aromatherapist will need to recognise.

REACTIONS TO TREATMENTS

Many of the reactions to aromatherapy treatment will be favourable, for example, improved mood, improved skin tone and texture, increased energy or relief from symptoms suffered. However, not all reactions experienced may be beneficial. When you use essential and carrier oils or other media on the skin you are introducing a foreign substance to the body. In some cases, the body may have an adverse or allergic reaction to the oils and this may show on the skin or in other systems of the body (e.g. sneezing or asthma). This section explains the most likely and common reactions. However, it is always advisable to be aware that other adverse irritations may occur and be able to recognise them.

Skin reactions

There are three main types of skin reactions.

- **cutaneous**

This common skin irritation is caused by a foreign substance reacting with the mast cells of the dermis. These cells respond by producing histamine which causes an inflammation of the skin. It is a local not whole body reaction. There are four main phases:

1. a localised wheal (raised, red mark) appears on contact with the substance (a common example of this is the spotty red nettle rash, also known as a form of urticaria)

2. generalised (whole body) urticaria, inflammation and pain

3. urticaria and bronchial asthma

4. urticaria and anaphylaxis (a state of shock which occurs as a result of an antigen-antibody reaction in the cells).

- **allergic/sensitivity**

This is a reaction of the immune system. When it first enters the skin, the foreign substance integrates with the lymphatic tissue and sensitises the T-lymphocytes. In the future, any contact with the same substance will cause the immune system to react and attack – this is an allergy. This attack usually causes skin irritations like those described above. Sometimes an allergy or hypersensitivity to a particular substance can be extremely fast and severe (nut allergies, for example, may prove fatal). Sensitising oils include benzoin, black pepper, clary sage, eucalyptus, jasmine absolute, juniper, pine, rose absolute, ylang ylang.

- **phototoxicity/photosensitisation**

This is a very common reaction to citrus oils. The foreign substance enters the skin and fuses with the cells. When the skin is later exposed to sunlight, it will be more sensitive and may burn and/or develop melanin disorders. Photosensitising oils include bergamot, ginger, lemon, mandarin, orange, patchouli.

Non-skin reactions

Any of the following may occur:
- asthma attacks
- migraines
- headaches
- severe nausea
- diarrhoea
- depression
- fatigue
- 'foggy' or 'muzzy' head.
- dizziness
- increase in frequency of micturition
- changes in appetite
- altered sleep patterns
- hyperactivity
- healing crisis

AROMATHERAPY MASSAGE

Most of these may be caused by overdoseage. The strength and concentration of essential oils is such that any mistakes in dilutions or blending may cause one or several of the above. If clients are planning to buy their own oils, it is very important to explain that they need to be used diluted not neat (there are very few exceptions). It is crucial to provide written instructions on correct use and safety implications.

How can reactions be prevented?
The first step is to take precautions by getting as much information from the client as possible and then giving them as much information as possible. This should be done in the first consultation. Any allergies to cosmetics, perfumes, toiletries, food or any family history of such allergies needs to be recorded. If any cosmetics or creams have been used on the area to be treated, especially the face and neck, the area will need to be cleansed. Any of the following will increase skin sensitivity:

- perfumes or perfumed products
- deodorants/antiperspirants
- aerobic/vigorous exercise or any activity that increases perspiration (because perspiration increases skin sensitivity).

If any cross-sensitisation or reaction occurs it must be recorded on the client card.

NB It is important to remember that –

- atopic clients (anyone who suffers from hayfever, allergic rhinitis, eczema, asthma, allergies to wool, dust or animal hair) are 13.5 times more likely to have a reaction to essential oils
- any history of melanoma or skins with large/dark moles are contra-indications for citrus oils which have been shown to increase malignancy rates.

- clients should be warned not to follow treatment with saunas, steambaths, sunbeds or beach sunbathing or waxing.

What if the aromatherapist is allergic or atopic?
The same precautions taken for clients should be taken by the aromatherapist, especially since the therapist will be spending long periods of time working with these concentrated substances. The following preventative measures should be used at all times:

- limit the amount of direct contact with neat oils.
- keep oils, both neat and diluted, away from the face and eyes. Hair should be tied up during massage but if a strand falls over the face, use the forearm to push it away from the face.
- between clients wash hands thoroughly and use an unperfumed moisture cream to protect them.
- if hands are sore or cracked do not use sensitising oils especially not absolutes which are known to cause more irritation due to the solvents used to extract them.
- limit personal use of perfumed products and cosmetics and limit exposure to household chemicals such as cleaning products/washing-up liquid (e.g. wear gloves when cleaning to protect hands). Cross-sensitisation may occur with constant exposure to perfumes or chemicals which react with the oils.

9 The holistic approach

In Brief

The first section of this chapter explains the holistic approach, integral biology and why they are important for practising aromatherapists; the second explains how a holistic approach and aromatherapy can help in the treatment of hospital and hospice patients.

Learning objectives

The target knowledge of this chapter is:
- the holistic approach
- integral biology
- the use of aromatherapy in hospitals, hospices, with the elderly and the terminally ill
- treatments suitable for use in a care setting.

WHAT IS THE HOLISTIC APPROACH?

The term holistic comes from the Greek word *holos* meaning whole. The holistic approach or treatment takes into account a person's whole being, not just the physical symptoms or problems but also psychology, environment and nutrition and the effects, both positive and negative, that these can have on the body as a whole.

What is integral biology?

Integral biology is the study of our environment's effect on our physical and mental health. Everything we do in our daily lives affects our bodies. For example, an uncomfortable working environment can cause stress, tiredness and related conditions such as anxiety, depression and heart conditions. At

Poor posture while sitting at a desk can cause digestive, muscular and skeletal problems.

home lack of exercise and a poor diet plus too much sedentary activity (watching TV, writing, reading, using computers) may cause similar problems.

What affects integral biology?

There are many factors that influence our integral biology. Some are negative and some positive.

Negative factors

- lack of exercise
- processed food
- chemically-treated fruit and vegetables
- lack of fresh air
- too much alcohol
- a stressful job
- bereavement or grief
- too much caffeine (tea, coffee, cola)
- lack of sleep
- financial problems
- worries about family
- worries about relationships
- too much time spent on or near electro-magnetic equipment (computers, photocopiers)
- smoky or poorly ventilated home or office
- internalising problems and worries.

Picking up heavy or awkward objects without bending the knees can damage the back.

Positive factors
- regular exercise
- eating fresh (preferably organic or non-chemically treated) fruit and vegetables
- a varied diet
- drinking lots of water
- taking regular breaks at work and home
- reorganising work patterns to avoid sitting or standing in the same place for several hours in a row
- getting enough sleep
- getting plenty of fresh air and making sure a window is open when someone is smoking.

How can these problems be treated by aromatherapy?

Imbalances in the external environment can cause imbalances internally. It is therefore important to take any apparently external factors into account before trying to treat physical symptoms. Poor circulation might appear to be a serious blood problem, but may be caused by lack of exercise and a diet lacking in nutrients. Aromatherapy aims to treat both the symptom and its real cause, not its probable one, in order to restore the body's equilibrium as quickly as possible.

How can an aromatherapist find out what is the real cause?

By careful questioning and discussion. When a client comes for a treatment the aromatherapist needs to find out as much as possible about the person and the problem (see Consultation Techniques in Chapter 8). Topics covered should include medical history, contra-indications to treatment, current illnesses or physical/psychological conditions,

family details, type of work and working conditions, stress at work and at home, hobbies, lifestyle (i.e. sedentary, active, relaxed, stressed), diet and exercise. The aromatherapist should also look for non-verbal clues such as nervous habits and poor posture that provide information on the patient's day-to-day life. On subsequent visits the aromatherapist should check for any changes and discuss these with the client before considering any adjustments of the oils and/or treatment methods used.

Can aromatherapy alone 'cure' the real cause once it is discovered?

In some cases yes. However, the aromatherapist may offer aftercare advice, explaining how aromatherapy is part of the process of healing and not a miracle cure and that if the conditions that caused the problem in the first place continue then the problem will continue as well. Also, it is important to remember that aromatherapy is complementary to traditional, or allopathic, medicine rather than a replacement for it. Where appropriate it can be used at the same time as traditional medicine.

Why is a holistic approach important?

Because it treats each person individually and in the context of their own life. This enables people to help themselves to improve their health and re-establish the body's equilibrium, known as homeostasis. Furthermore, for the best therapeutic effect and the most accurate choice of oils for a treatment, all aspects of integral biology need to be considered.

You now know about the holistic approach and integral biology. The next section explains how aromatherapy may be used in a care setting such as a hospital or hospice.

THE CAUSES OF STRESS AND ITS EFFECTS

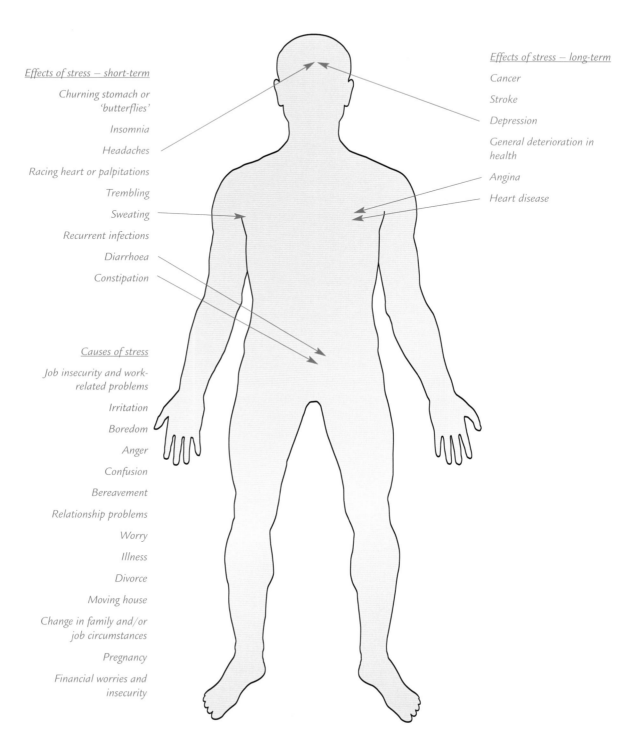

Effects of stress – short-term

Churning stomach or 'butterflies'

Insomnia

Headaches

Racing heart or palpitations

Trembling

Sweating

Recurrent infections

Diarrhoea

Constipation

Causes of stress

Job insecurity and work-related problems

Irritation

Boredom

Anger

Confusion

Bereavement

Relationship problems

Worry

Illness

Divorce

Moving house

Change in family and/or job circumstances

Pregnancy

Financial worries and insecurity

Effects of stress – long-term

Cancer

Stroke

Depression

General deterioration in health

Angina

Heart disease

Causes of stress and its effects.

What is stress?

Stress is any factor that threatens our physical or mental well-being. Such factors can be imagined (worry about the future) or real (financial problems). It is not the factor itself that is damaging but the response to it. Some people have very stressful lives but manage stress so that it does not affect them whereas for others even the slightest worry can have damaging consequences.

How does stress affect us?

The body has always had to respond to stress. Thousands of years ago, stress factors were more physical: humans needed to hunt for their food, protect themselves from wild animals and secure shelter. In the twenty-first century stress factors are likely to be more intangible: job insecurity, worrying about relationship difficulties, irritation about traffic jams. However, the effects of stress are exactly the same whether the threat is an angry boss or an angry buffalo! The body, perceiving danger, prepares to face it or run away (the fight or flight syndrome). Several systems shut down and the body works to conserve energy to enable movement and escape: adrenaline rushes into the body to warn of impending danger and the heart rate increases, the blood vessels contract increasing blood pressure, the digestive functions shut down and the muscles contract.

If the perceived danger is then removed or escapes, the stress response has achieved its aim and the body relaxes. However, usually, it is not easy to get away from the cause of the stress. Most stress factors are no longer responded to with activity: it is very hard for an office worker to run away from an annoying problem or colleague. As a result the body remains tense and cannot relax. It is this unused response mechanism which is damaging.

How is stress damaging?

It has been estimated that stress is the cause of 75% of disease. In the short term, as a response to perceived danger, stress is literally life-saving. If we didn't feel stress we would not make the effort to cross the road a little faster to get out of the way of an approaching car, or perform at a heightened rate in a sports match or competition in order to win. However, in the long term, if a person continues to feel stress in response to external factors but does nothing either to remove the cause of the stress or to respond to it differently, the stress reaction can be damaging. The body remains in a state of alert and eventually this will have a physical effect on the systems concerned.

What are the symptoms of stress?

Anyone who has ever been nervous about an interview, exam, meeting or important football match has felt some of the symptoms of stress.

These include: churning stomach or 'butterflies', racing heart or palpitations, diarrhoea, loss of appetite, trembling, insomnia, sweating. In the medium term these symptoms, left untreated, may cause chest pains, allergies, persistent insomnia, high blood pressure, abdominal pain, migraines, depression, ulcers, asthma and infections. In the long term constant stress is known to cause heart disease, strokes, cancer, angina and may be fatal.

How can stress be cured?

Stress in itself cannot be 'cured' because threats to our well-being will always exist around us. However, it is not the threat but the way it is perceived and responded to that is most important. If stress is managed it is no longer damaging, e.g. if stuck in traffic, one driver may become enraged whereas another will accept that this is a normal situation in a busy area. The first driver is responding to stress, the second is managing it. However, the actual stress factor itself is the same.

How can stress be managed?

By learning to respond in a healthier way and using relaxation techniques. We cannot simply tell our bodies to relax; we have to learn how to relax them, via particular relaxing activities as well as with specific breathing, visualisation and relaxation techniques.

How can aromatherapy help

When the body is stressed it must work harder than usual in order to remain balanced. Hence, stressed people tend to over-use conventional relaxation methods such as drinking and smoking in order to reach the same calm as the less stressed. Aromatherapy brings the body back into balance, restoring homeostasis and inducing deep relaxation which helps to remove the pent-up tension of the stress response. It boosts the immune system, which is weakened by constant stress, stimulates the circulation, removes toxins, stabilises breathing, boosts energy levels and induces calm in both mind and body. As a one-off it can help the body to recover from stress; as a continuous treatment or series of treatments it can help the client to learn how to relax and therefore how to manage the stress that caused the problem in the first place. The use of essences and fixed oils as part of a specific homecare routine, reinforce the beneficial effects of a professional treatment programme, allowing the client to incorporate oils into an ongoing holistic lifestyle.

Oils that help with stress related conditions

The following oils are thought to be useful when treating clients with stress related conditions such as nervous tension and anxiety as well as the physiological effects of stress such as muscular tension:

Basil, benzoin, bergamot, cedarwood, German chamomile, Roman chamomile, clary sage, cypress, frankincense, geranimum, jasmine, juniper, lavender (angustifolia), lemongrass, mandarin, marjoram, peppermint, bitter orange, sweet orange, neroli, patchouli, petitgrain, rose cabbage, rose damask, sandalwood, thyme, vetiver, ylang ylang. However, a full consultation may reveal many signs and symptoms that need to be addressed. The aromatherapist will need to take all aspects of the client's health and lifestyle into consideration to blend the correct synergistic mix of oils and recommend the most suitable methods of application for an effective treatment programme.

You now know what stress is and how aromatherapy can be used to combat it. The final section in this chapter explains how aromatherapy may be used in a care setting such as a hospital or hospice.

THE USE OF AROMATHERAPY IN A CARE SETTING

How can aromatherapy be used in health care?

Essential oils can benefit health on physical, psychological and pharmacological levels and are thus very suitable for use in a health care environment. When ill or hospitalised, one or more of the patient's five senses may be affected. Smell is a powerful stimulant, both of the memory and the rest of the body and thus aromatherapy's combination of aromas and touch can enhance the life of a patient to great effect. With the advent of antibiotic-resistant 'superbugs' research is being undertaken using essential oils to prevent bacterial growth and assist in cases where body tissue is slow to heal.

When is it not suitable?

Using aromatherapy in any way requires communication between the medical practitioner, therapist and patient. The therapist needs to know of any contraindications to treatment and prescription medicines the patient is taking. The aromatherapist can ask the doctor to sign a letter of consent specifying the type of treatment to be performed. Some healthcare trusts decline written permission due to an increase in litigation but many doctors feel that their patients are able to take decisions about their own health.

What precautions need to be taken in this environment?

Therapists who are able to work in a care setting should be aware of and comply with any existing care plans, should keep detailed consultation forms and records and blend oils and use with care and consideration. Some establishments require that oils mixed for patients are kept with other drugs, usually in a cabinet or on a locked trolley so that their use is recorded. All blends must be fully documented and agreed with the client or client's advocate. Endorsement of the agreed blend must be noted on the consultation form with the client/advocate's signature.

Is it available on the NHS?

Aromatherapy is not, at the time of writing, fully available through NHS doctors and hospitals, but many practices and private hospitals offer it as a service which patients may pay for if they wish. There are, however, several pioneering hospitals which offer aromatherapy to both patients and staff.

Is aromatherapy suitable for people with special needs or learning difficulties?

The use of essential oils in this particular setting is becoming more widespread. Aromatherapy is often used in combination with specialised units such as Snoozelum rooms to enhance development and calm behaviour. Patients sometimes suffer physical problems caused by their repetitive or limited movements and the application of oils like lavender have been used to help heal and protect the skin. Benefits include improved sleep patterns and a relaxation of physical tetany (muscle spasms).

Can aromatherapy be used with the elderly?

This sector of care is enlarging dramatically as more people live on into their 80s and 90s. The traditional role of the family as carers has changed and this task is now being undertaken by professionals. Aromatherapy is particularly applicable here as many elderly people suffer the stress of bereavement, loss of their home, moving to a new area, making new friends often coupled with ill health. Loss of physical contact also plays a large part as people age and become withdrawn as a result of change. Aromatherapy works on many levels and can be used to help both physical and psychological health problems.

Can aromatherapy help the terminally ill?

Extensive research into the effects of aromatherapy in a palliative care environment (for the terminally ill) is being carried out. Essential oils are used to provide pain relief, lessen the side effects of other treatments and combat the stress experienced by patients suffering terminal illness and their families. Several programmes exist in hospitals and healthcare trusts where the importance of stress reduction, alternative pain relief and simple human contact have been recognised. Some general hospitals are also using aromatherapy for palliative care.

Which treatments are suitable in hospital?

Essential oils may be used in a care setting in many ways:

- **massage** – limited body movement due to health problems may prevent full body massage, but massaging parts of the body that are accessible can bring about a feeling of relaxation and temporary relief from pain. Patients who cannot move around a lot particularly suffer from poor blood and lymphatic circulation and aromatherapy massage can help stimulate these. The therapist should take into account any prescribed medication and possible contra-indications when selecting oils and

blending for massage. Carrier oils also need to be selected carefully as patients may have more delicate skin as a result of medication, constant wear and tear or age and some of the heavier fixed oils may be too sticky for massage use.

- **compresses** – both hot and cold compresses may be used to ease painful joints, aching muscles or cool a fevered brow. For methods, see Chapter 7 – Application.

- **foot/hand baths** – useful for people who can't move around, yet want to experience the benefits of hydrotherapy and aromatherapy. Hot or cold water may be used and specific oils chosen depending on the patient's requirements.

- **inhalation** – the simplest method. One or two drops of oil may be put on a tissue for the patient to inhale. This method is often very useful for emotional conditions such as stress, depression or anxiety and it is also extremely portable – the patient can take the tissue wherever they go and continue inhaling the oil. Inhalation also allows the patient to choose the oils they wish to use.

- **burners/vaporisers/diffusers** – care must be taken when recommending the use of burners. The use of naked flames in a care setting is prohibited so standard essential oil burners are not suitable; however electric burners can be used. These make use of a sealed electric coil under a clay or glazed ceramic bowl. The essential oil is placed in the bowl and then the burner is turned on. Oil may also be placed in the bowl with a tiny amount of water, but the vaporiser needs to be unplugged first. As with a normal burner, electric burners get very hot and need to be placed on a heatproof mat. As the coil heats, the oil vaporises into the air. Care should be taken to ensure electrical safety – no trailing wires and do not place the vaporiser near water. Manufacturers' instructions must be followed at all times. Equipment is also available in the form of nebulisers, diffusers or vaporisers that use a pump to blow out a very fine mist of oil into the air. Again, manufacturers' instructions for use must be followed carefully. All electrical equipment must be subject to regular electrical safety checks in line with the insurance requirements of the care establishment. If the patient's immune system has been weakened, vaporisers are of great use with antiviral oils. Electric burners can be switched off and remain warm for hours, thereby continuing the vaporisation. Light bulb rings are also suitable if used correctly.

Are there any oils that are particularly helpful in this setting?

Patients finding themselves in a hospital, nursing/residential home, hospice, or rehabilitation unit are often stressed as a result of changes in their health and home environment. This may show physically or mentally; anxiety, depression, frustration and anger are common as are muscle and joint pains, headaches, digestive disorders, oedema and circulatory problems. Some useful oils for treating these problems are listed below and the A–Z in Chapter 6 provides information on specific oils.

Anxiety/depression/stress
Basil, benzoin, bergamot, chamomile (Roman), clary sage, cypress, frankincense, geranium, jasmine, lavender, mandarin, melissa, neroli, patchouli, petitgrain, rose, rosewood, sandalwood, sweet marjoram, vetiver, ylang ylang.

Grief/bereavement
Benzoin, chamomile (Roman), cypress, geranium, lavender, mandarin, melissa, neroli, patchouli, rose, sweet marjoram, myrrh, vetiver.

Wounds/scars/skin healing
Bergamot, chamomile (Roman and blue German), cypress, eucalyptus, frankincense, geranium, juniper, lavender, lemon, myrrh, patchouli, tea tree.

Muscular problems
Black pepper, cypress, clary sage, ginger, grapefruit, lavender, lemongrass, sweet marjoram, rosemary, thyme.

Joint problems
Benzoin, black pepper, chamomile (Roman and blue German), eucalyptus, ginger, juniper, lavender, lemon, myrrh, pine, sage, thyme, vetiver.

DON'T FORGET TO USE YOUR RESOURCE CD ROM

■ TEST YOUR KNOWLEDGE OF ESSENTIAL OILS

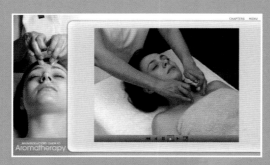

■ TEST YOUR KNOWLEDGE QUESTIONS

■ FULL VIDEO OF PRACTICAL SKILLS

AND MUCH MORE!

An introductory guide to Aromatherapy

10 Other complementary therapies

In Brief

Aromatherapy is only one of many complementary and holistic therapies. This chapter gives a brief overview of others. Some aromatherapy therapists combine therapies in treatment. For example massage and acupressure which are both compatible with aromatherapy treatments

Learning objectives ●

The target knowledge of this chapter is:
● the definition of other complementary therapies.

OTHER COMPLEMENTARY THERAPIES

OTHER COMPLEMENTARY THERAPIES

Acupressure

Acupressure is the same as acupunture but with the use of thumb or knuckles rather than needles. Pressure is applied along meridians to release the body's own energy – chi – to help relieve pain and encourage the body to heal itself. The massage is similar to Shiatsu, but performed directly onto the skin with the use of a light oil or talc.

Acupuncture

An ancient Chinese therapy, now being used increasingly in the West, acupuncture is the insertion of very fine needles into the skin at certain points to help relieve pain and improve the body's own healing mechanisms. The points are on meridians (energy channels). If there is a blockage in energy then a part of the body connected to that meridian may become ill or weak. The needles are thought to release the blockage and help the body to heal itself.

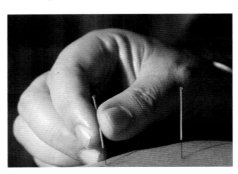

Alexander technique

The Alexander technique encourages healing and better health through better posture and awareness of how the body is used. It is especially useful for backache and headaches. It was developed by an actor called Frederick Mathias Alexander who discovered that improving his posture stopped him losing his voice.

Bach flower remedies

Dr Edward Bach, a doctor and a practising homeopath, turned away from both traditional medicine and homeopathy believing that there was a more natural and holistic way to treat illness. He developed these thirty-eight remedies, which are infusions of plants with water and alcohol, based on his research in the countryside. The remedies aim to treat mental and emotional problems, which often precede and cause physical symptoms.

Bowen technique

The Bowen technique, developed in Australia by Thomas A. Bowen, aims to rebalance the body holistically using gentle moves on tissues. A Bowen practitioner can feel whether muscles are stressed or tense and use the moves to release this build-up. The light rolling movements stimulate the body's energy flows. It is not a massage or a manipulation but a gentle process that encourages the body to heal itself.

Chiropractic

A chiropractor manipulates the joints of the body, specifically the spine, in order to relieve pain. It works on the basis that pain is often caused by a nerve which is not functioning properly and thus the spine, through which the central nervous system runs, is the focus of the therapy. It is especially useful for lower back and neck pain as well as headaches.

Herbalism

Herbalism is the use of plants, usually the whole plant, to make herbal remedies. It is an ancient, traditional medicine — what is now considered 'traditional medicine' only replaced it in the last three hundred years.

Holistic Massage

These techniques use classical Swedish massage techniques to treat physical and psychological problems. Routines usually cover the body and can include movements performed on the face and scalp. Pressure varies depending on the area of the body being worked upon and client requirements.

Homeopathy

Homeopathy treats like with like. By using minute doses of the bacteria, virus or substance which has caused the problem in the first place (i.e. cat hair in a remedy for an allergy to cat hairs) the treatment builds up the patient's resistance and immunity to the problem, substance or bacteria. Many homeopathic remedies have to be used and even stored well away from strong smells because such smells can reduce their effectiveness.

Indian Head Massage

A traditional form of head massage, using specific techniques covering only the head, neck and upper back. This treatment is very effective in treating stress, headaches and eyestrain.

Infant and Child Massage

The massage of babies and young children, usually performed by the parent, to calm, soothe and help with conditions such as colic. This incorporates techniques such as effleurage and petrissage using light pressure.

Iridology

By studying the irises (the coloured parts of the eyes) of a patient and noting any changes, iridologists can diagnose physical and psychological problems.

Kinesiology

Kinesiology is an holistic treatment that focuses on testing the muscles and energy meridians to discover and then treat the body's imbalances on all levels: chemically, energetically, physically and mentally. Using different positions and the application of pressure to the limbs, the kinesiologist can determine whether there are any energy blocks in the body and correct them through firm massage. Kinesiology is preventative and, like many complementary therapies, aims to treat the whole person.

Osteopathy

Like a chiropractor, an osteopath manipulates the joints of the body. Osteopaths work on the basis that the body's structure and function are interdependent: if the structure is damaged in any way it will affect the function. By manipulating joints and bones they can correct structural problems which will improve the body's function.

Physiotherapy

Physiotherapy uses physical exercises, massage and the application of pressure to relieve physical pain and muscular tension. It is often used to re-educate the body in cases of major surgery, illness, or an accident.

Reiki

Reiki means universal life force energy in Japanese. Reiki healers act as channels for this universal energy to pass into the patient. By using hands in certain positions on different parts of the body, the healer is said to draw energy to the body, promoting healing, balance and relaxation.

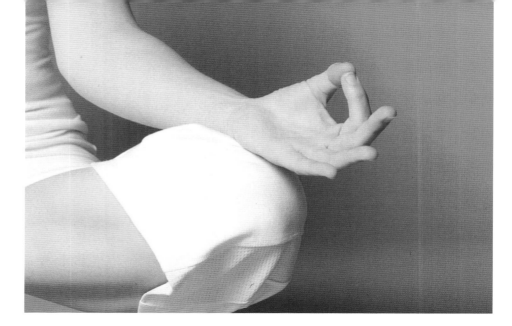

Reflexology

This holistic therapy treats the whole person, particularly weak or ill areas, by using the feet as 'maps' of the body. On the feet there are points or zones which correspond to organs and systems of the body. By pressing on one of these points, the corresponding organ in the body is affected. For example, pressing on the tip of the big toe will cause a response in the brain and, vice versa, if there is a problem with the brain the reflexologist will recognise the symptoms of this in the big toe. This relationship, between a point on the foot and another part of the body is known as a reflex. A trained reflexologist uses finger or thumb pressure on each of the zones to find the problem areas. He or she then applies more pressure which helps the corresponding part of the body to heal. Some professionals use reflexology techniques during massage treatment.

Shiatsu

Shiatsu is a form of acupressure: the use of finger or thumb pressure on points along meridians (energy channels) to help relieve pain and encourage the body to heal itself. The pressure points are the same as those used in acupuncture. It is performed with the client clothed.

Thai massage

A traditional form of bodywork, where the Thai massage therapist uses yoga movements, pressure and stretches to balance body energy. Performed with the client clothed and positioned on a mat on the floor.

Yoga/Meditation

Both yoga and meditation have long been known to have beneficial, holistic effects and they are very useful self-help therapies. They teach the learner to have control of the body and mind. Yoga does this through physical exercise, including adopting different postures, relaxation techniques and breathing exercises. Meditation uses different focuses (such as visualisation, a candle or a mantra) to help a person find calm and a sense of their own centre. Meditation has the physiological effects of a short sleep, i.e. the body goes into the healing and recharging mode it adopts when we sleep, allowing the muscles to relax and the circulation to become more efficient.

You now know details of several other complementary therapies.

11 Case studies

In Brief

Practising aromatherapists keep detailed notes about clients' treatments: their reasons for choosing aromatherapy massage, the oils used to treat the condition or problem and the reactions to and results of treatment. This final chapter provides an insight into this treatment process

NB Any names and certain details have been changed to preserve privacy. Medical history would also have been checked in detail.

CLIENT LIFESTYLE/PROFILE

Mrs CD is 46 years old. She works as a canine beautician. She was diagnosed with multiple sclerosis in 1999. She is in good health considering her condition, but she has experienced relapses approximately once every three years since diagnosis, but the last time she experienced one was five years ago. She underwent a hysterectomy in 2003. She now takes medication daily to help with menopausal symptoms. She has suffered blackouts and fits in the past and her GP suspected epilepsy. However, he now feels that they were probably as a result of the MS and she has not suffered any for at least ten years. She is on no other medication.

She has to be extremely careful and manage her energy levels. She takes two days off per week and often works late. She experiences extreme fatigue and other distressing symptoms like widespread aches and pains if she overworks.

She is married with two children, one of whom still lives at home. Her husband also suffers ill health and is unable to work which puts a great financial strain on them both.

She would like to try aromatherapy to see if it will boost her energy levels and immune system. It may also help with the anxiety and mild depression she experiences, as well as providing some stress relief.

Her GP has been consulted with regard to the aromatherapy treatments and he has given his written approval for treatment to proceed.

Treatment plan

One aromatherapy massage per week for four weeks; working on full body and face, together with suitable recommendations for Home care/self treatment. The emphasis of the massage and movements used will be for relaxation and absorption of the oils so I will concentrate on using effleurage and lymphatic drainage movements. Pressure points will be used to relieve tension and congestion in specific areas such as the back and face.

Conditions to treat and suitable essences/essential oils

Mild depression/anxiety/nervous system
Basil (Lamiaceae, Ocimum basilicum),

Client Consultation Form – Aromatherapy

College Name:
College Number:
Student Name:
Student Number:
Date: Feb

Client Name: Mrs CD
Address: Hampshire

Profession: Canine Beautician
Tel. No: Day
                     Eve

PERSONAL DETAILS

Age group: ❏ Under 20   ❏ 20–30   ❏ 30–40   ☑ 40–50   ❏ 50–60   ❏ 60+
Lifestyle: ☑ Active   ❏ Sedentary   **GP Address:** Hampshire
Last visit to the doctor: 6 months ago   **No. of children (if applicable):** 2
                                                                   Date of last period (if applicable): n/a

CONTRAINDICATIONS REQUIRING MEDICAL PERMISSION – in circumstances where medical permission cannot be obtained clients must give their informed consent in writing prior to treatment (select where/if appropriate):

❏ Pregnancy (use only mandarin)
❏ Cardiovascular conditions (thrombosis, phlebitis, hypertension, hypotension, heart conditions)
❏ Haemophilia
❏ Any condition already being treated by a GP or another complementary practitioner
❏ Medical oedema
❏ Osteoporosis
❏ Arthritis
❏ Nervous/Psychotic conditions
❏ Epilepsy
❏ Recent operations
❏ Diabetes
❏ Asthma
☑ Any dysfunction of the nervous system (e.g. Multiple

Sclerosis, Parkinson's disease, Motor neurone disease)
❏ Bells Palsy
❏ Trapped/Pinched nerve (e.g. sciatica)
❏ Inflamed nerve
❏ Cancer
❏ Spastic conditions
❏ Kidney infections
❏ Hormonal implants
❏ Undiagnosed pain
☑ When taking prescribed medication
❏ Acute rheumatism
❏ Whiplash
❏ Slipped disc
❏ Cervical spondylitis

N.B. All known allergies should be checked
Client contraindications should be checked against the safety data for each oil prior to treatment

CONTRAINDICTIONS THAT RESTRICT TREATMENT (select where/if appropriate):

❏ Fever
❏ Contagious or infectious diseases
❏ Under the influence of alcohol or recreational drugs
❏ Diarrhoea and vomiting
❏ Skin diseases
❏ Undiagnosed lumps and bumps
❏ Localised swelling
❏ Inflammation
❏ Varicose veins
❏ Pregnancy (abdomen)
❏ Breast feeding
❏ Cuts
❏ Bruises

❏ Abrasions
❏ Scar tissue (2 years for major operation and 6 months for a small scar)
❏ Sunburn
❏ Abdomen (first few days of menstruation depending how the client feels)
❏ Haematoma
❏ Recent fractures (minimum 3 months)
❏ Gastric ulcers
❏ Hernia
❏ After a heavy meal
❏ Hypersensitive skin

WRITTEN PERMISSION REQUIRED BY:

☑ GP/Specialist   ❏ Informed consent
Either of which should be attached to the consultation form.

PERSONAL INFORMATION (select if/where appropriate):

Muscular/Skeletal problems: ☐ Back ☑ Aches/Pain ☐ Stiff joints ☐ Headaches

Digestive problems: ☐ Constipation ☐ Bloating ☐ Liver/Gall bladder ☐ Stomach

Circulation: ☐ Heart ☐ Blood pressure ☐ Fluid retention ☐ Tired legs ☐ Varicose veins
☐ Cellulite ☐ Kidney problems ☐ Cold hands and feet

Gynaecological: ☐ Irregular periods ☐ P.M.T ☑ Menopause ☑ H.R.T ☐ Pill ☐ Coil
Other: ....

Nervous system: ☐ Migraine ☐ Tension ☑ Stress ☑ Depression
....

Immune system: ☑ Prone to infections ☐ Sore throats ☐ Colds ☐ Chest ☐ Sinuses
....

Regular antibiotic/medication taken? ☐ Yes ☑ No
....

Herbal remedies taken? ☐ Yes ☑ No
....

Ability to relax: ☐ Good ☑ Moderate ☐ Poor

Sleep patterns: ☐ Good ☑ Poor ☐ Average No. of hours 6

Do you see natural daylight in your workplace? ☑ Yes ☐ No

Do you work at a computer? ☐ Yes ☑ No If yes how many hours

Do you eat regular meals? ☑ Yes ☐ No

Do you eat in a hurry? ☑ Yes ☐ No

Do you take any food/vitamin supplements? ☐ Yes ☑ No
If yes, which ones: ....

How many portions of each of these items does your diet contain per day?
Fresh fruit: 1 Fresh vegetables: 3 Protein: 2 source?
Dairy produce: 3 Sweet things: 2 Added salt: 0 Added sugar: 2

How many units of these drinks do you consume per day?
Tea: 3 Coffee: 2 Fruit juice: 1 Water: 0 Soft drinks: 0 Others: 0

Do you suffer from food allergies? ☐ Yes ☑ No Bingeing? ☐ Yes ☑ No
Overeating? ☐ Yes ☑ No

Do you suffer from eating disorders? Bingeing? ☐ Yes ☑ No Overeating? ☐ Yes ☐ No

Under eating ☐ Yes ☐ No

Do you smoke? ☐ No ☑ Yes How many per day? 1–5

Do you drink alcohol? ☐ No ☑ Yes How many units per day? 1

Do you exercise? ☐ None ☑ Occasional ☐ Irregular ☐ Regular
Types: ....

What is your skin type? ☐ Dry ☐ Oil ☑ Combination ☐ Sensitive ☐ Dehydrated

Do you suffer/have you suffered from: ☐ Dermatitis ☐ Acne ☐ Eczema ☐ Psoriasis
....

☐ Allergies ☐ Hay Fever ☐ Asthma ☐ Skin cancer

Stress level: 1–10 (10 being the highest)
At work 8 At home 8

CASE STUDIES

Bergamot (Rutaceae, Citrus bergamia), Roman Chamomile (Asteraceae, Chamaemelum nobile), German Chamomile (Asteraceae, Matricaria recutica), Cedarwood Atlas (Pinaceae, Cedrus atlantica)), Clary Sage (Lamiaceae, Salvia sclarea), Cypress (Cupressaceae, Cupressus sempervirens), Frankincense (Burseraceae, Boswellia sacra), Geranium (Geraniaceae, Pelargonium graveolens), Jasmine (Oleaceae, Jasminum grandiflorum), Lavender (Lamiaceae, Lavandula angustifolia), Lemon (Rutaceae, Citrus limon), Mandarin (Rutaceae, Citrus nobilis), Neroli (Rutaceae, Citrus aurantium), Patchouli (Lamiaceae, Pogostemon cablin), Rose damask (Rosaceae, Rosa damascena), Marjoram (Lamiaceae, Origanum majorana).

Stress/immune system

Basil (Lamiaceae, Ocimum basilicum), Bergamot (Rutaceae, Citrus bergamia), Geranium (Geraniaceae, Pelargonium graveolens), Lavender (Lamiaceae, Lavandula angustifolia), Neroli (Rutaceae, Citrus aurantium), Petitgrain (Rutaceae, Citrus aurantium), Marjoram (Lamiaceae, Origanum majorana).

Menopausal symptoms

Bergamot (Rutaceae, Citrus bergamia), Roman Chamomile (Asteraceae, Chamaemelum nobile), German

Chamomile(Asteraceae, Matricaria recutica) , Cypress(Cupressaceae, Cupressus sempervirens), Geranium (Geraniaceae, Pelargonium graveolens), Clary Sage (Lamiaceae, Salvia sclarea), Rose damask (Rosaceae, Rosa damascena), Ylang Ylang (Annonaceae, Canaga odorata), Jasmine(Oleaceae, Jasminum grandiflorum), Neroli (Rutaceae, Citrus aurantium).

Muscular aches and pains

Basil (Lamiaceae, Ocimum basilicum), Ginger (Zingiberaceae, Zingiber officinale), Marjoram (Lamiaceae, Origanum majorana), Lavender (Lamiaceae, Lavandula angustifolia), Roman Chamomile(Asteraceae, Chamaemelum nobile), Peppermint (Lamiaceae, Mentha piperita), Juniper (Cupressaceae, Juniperus communis), Thyme (Lamiaceae, Thymus vulgaris).

Oils to avoid (epilepsy)

Eucalyptus (Myrtaceae, Eucalyptus globulus) Fennel (Apiaceae, Foeniculum vulgare), Rosemary (Lamiaceae, Rosmarinus officinalis)

Fixed oils

Almond Oil (Rosaceae, Prunus communis), Evening Primrose Oil (Onagraceae, Oenothera biennis), Jojoba (Simmondsiaceae, Simmondsia chinensis)

TREATMENT 1   08/02

Treatment Plan

Mrs CD arrived for treatment after a very busy day. She appeared tense and said she was achy and tired. The treatment took place in the early evening so relaxing oils were chosen to soothe her active mind and prepare her for sleep later. Pain relief and relaxation were the aims of the treatment this evening.

Rationale for the choice of each essence

Marjoram (Lamiaceae, Origanum majorana, Alcohols) – Muscular aches and pains, stress relief, depression
Geranium (Geraniaceae, Pelargonium graveolens, Alcohols) – Support immune system, depression
Lavender (Lamiaceae, Lavandula

angustifolia, Esters) – Healing to skin (spots on client's face), aches and pains, depression, anxiety

Rationale for choice of each fixed oil

Almond Oil was chosen for its nourishing properties. Mrs CD's skin was slightly dry on the body and she did not have a nut allergy. Evening Primrose Oil was also chosen as it contains GLA – an essential fatty acid and is suitable for the face.

Alternative oils that could have been used

Bergamot – Uplifting, immune system
Rose damask– Anti-depressant, relaxing, sedative
Clary Sage – Muscle relaxant, uplifting

Ratio of blending

Body

15mls Almond Oil, 5 mls Evening Primrose Oil
4 drops – Marjoram
2 drops – Geranium
1 drop – Lavender

Face

5 mls Evening Primrose Oil
1 drop - Lavender

Client feedback

She relaxed quite quickly and almost fell asleep. Tension was felt in the shoulders/upper back.

Aftercare/home care advice

Mrs CD was given a glass of water to drink whilst I went through the after/home care advice with her. She needs to drink plenty of water as she does not drink much each day. We also discussed potential reactions to the treatment. She was advised that these should all pass within 24 hours and that they are quite normal reactions to treatment.

Mrs CD cannot use a vaporiser at work because of the dogs, so I suggested 2 drops of Peppermint oil on a tissue for inhalation during the day if feeling fatigued.
She could also use Geranium oil in the bath – 3 drops in a tablespoon of milk added to a full bath of warm, not hot, water, approximately twice per week.

Self Reflection

I was wary of the overuse of oils with this client, as I did not want to overload a potentially sensitive system. As I was slightly worried about potential reactions to treatment, I did not want to advise the use of oils too often initially. Mrs CD expressed a preference for flowery odours after trying some of the oils and I selected lavender and geranium. However my oil choice was slightly limited due to the suspected epilepsy. It was quite daunting working on someone with a serious health problem. As the client felt quite achy and fatigued, I increased the number of drops of Marjoram to help with the muscular aches and pains and used plenty of effleurage to warm the tissues and promote oil absorption. When I applied the pressure points either side of the spine, she felt some discomfort particularly in the lower back so I eased the pressure applied as I continued. She relaxed well and appeared to enjoy the treatment.

TREATMENT 2   16/02

Treatment Plan

Another evening session. Mrs CD said that she was looking forward to relaxing. She was less achy even though she had groomed lots of dogs. Relaxation, stress relief, mood lifting, and immune system support were the treatment aims. Mrs CD said that she had felt a bit low this week, possibly as a result of doing too much. Her facial skin seemed a little clearer, so Bergamot was chosen to uplift rather than Lavender

Rationale for choice of each essence

Clary Sage (Lamiaceae, Salvia sclarea, Esters)– Managing menopause, relaxing, stress relief, uplifting
Geranium (Geraniaceae, Pelargonium graveolens, Alcohols) – Immune system support, depression
Bergamot (Rutaceae, Citrus bergamia, Esters) –Depression, anxiety, combination skin, immune system

Rationale for choice of each fixed oil

Almond Oil was chosen for its nourishing properties. Evening Primrose Oil was also chosen as it contains GLA and is light oil for the face.

Alternative oils

Rose damask – Antidepressant, relaxing sedative
Ylang Ylang – Antidepressant, sedative
Basil – Fatigue, antidepressant, nervine
Thyme – Antispasmodic, tonic, immune system

Ratio of blending
Body
15ml Almond Oil and 5ml Evening Primrose Oil
3 drops – Clary Sage
3 drops – Geranium
1 drop – Bergamot

Face
5ml Evening Primrose Oil
1 drop – Bergamot

Client Feedback

Mrs CD had gone to bed early after the last treatment. The next day, she had a headache that lasted all day. She had used the Geranium oil once in the bath and said it made her feel relaxed but not sleepy. Mrs CD was tense in her lower back but she had been working hard this week. She did not report any noticeable backache however. Her main concern this week was her mood. She said she felt quite 'down' but could not explain why. She relaxed well but did not fall asleep and talked for a little while about her day. She grew quiet as the treatment progressed.

Aftercare/home care advice

She felt thirsty after the treatment and quickly drank the water provided. Mrs CD was keen to use oils for inhalation as I mentioned that this could help raise her spirits or clear her head. Petitgrain and Peppermint were recommended. Whilst she cannot use the oils in a vaporiser at work, she can use them at home in the evenings to relax and wind down from a busy day – Lavender, Marjoram or Clary Sage were recommended. She was given the correct advice on how to use a vaporiser.

Self Reflection

Mrs CD relaxed well. It took quite a while to select the oils for this treatment. It is important to select oils the client likes as they would become conscious of an odour they dislike and not relax fully as a result. I also had to spend more time massaging her lower back so adjusted my treatment timing. I remembered that she had found the pressure points uncomfortable either side of her lower back so I applied less pressure there to start and then increased it to a level that she was comfortable with. My hands felt a little stiff when I applied the lymphatic drainage movements on the legs, but I am sure that this will improve with practice.

TREATMENT 3   24/02

Treatment Plan

Mrs CD arrived looking very tired. She had to go to a meeting later in the evening so she needed something that would revive her, as she needed to be alert to take minutes. She had experienced a busy week and worked late one day. This had upset her whole week, and she had been struggling to catch up ever since. Her MS symptoms have not been a problem, and she is feeling reasonably well. We tested several oils before deciding on the final blend. Treatment aims were to uplift, relieve stress and support the immune system.

Rationale for the choice of each essence

Basil (Lamiaceae, Ocimum basilicum, Alcohols) – Antidepressant, cephalic, nervine, muscular aches and pains
Lemon (Rutaceae, Citrus limon, Monoterpenes) – Immunostimulant, tonic, uplifting
Geranium (Geraniaceae, Pelargonium graveolens, Alcohols) – Uplifting, astringent

Rationale for choice of each fixed oil

Almond Oil was chosen for its nourishing properties and I have used it successfully in previous treatments. Mrs CD's facial skin is slightly drier this week so I will use Almond oil on the face in place of the Evening Primrose Oil.

Alternative oils that could have been used

Grapefruit – Antidepressant, stimulant
Juniper   – Analgesic, stimulant, tonic
 Lemongrass - Antidepressant, stimulant, uplifting, tonic

Ratio of blending

Body
20mls Almond Oil
3 drops – Basil
3 drops – Lemon
1 drop – Geranium

Face
5mls Almond Oil
1 drop – Geranium

Client Feedback

She felt really relaxed after the last treatment and slept well afterwards. The next day she felt 'groggy' and tired all day. This did not last. As a result, she said that she would like to relax but not quite as much! She did almost fall asleep at one point, even though the blend was supposed to invigorate her. Her skin seemed a little drier this evening and absorbed the oil quite quickly. After the treatment she looked brighter and said that she felt good and less tired.

Aftercare/home care advice

I advised her to drink plenty of water and gave her a few drops of Basil and Lemon mixed in a bottle to use on either a tissue or in her vaporiser as needed and discussed previously.

CASE STUDIES

TREATMENT 3 continued

Self Reflection

I was actually surprised by this blend – we worked through several oils before Mrs CD found one that was acceptable. I originally thought that it was too harsh and tried to recommend some other oils but Mrs CD really liked it, and seemed very upbeat after the treatment. I must learn to guide the client sensitively in their choice of oils and not try to select oils that I prefer. Mrs CD does not seem to be suffering any MS symptoms at the moment, only fatigue. My pressure point application is more specific now and Mrs CD is quite happy with the pressure. For stress relief I think that this routine is more beneficial, the effleurage movements seem to calm the client down quickly and the oils are helping with muscular aches and pains.

TREATMENT 4   02/03

Treatment Plan

Mrs CD arrived and seemed in a good mood. She said that she was sad that this was our last treatment session, as she looked forward to them. She has not experienced any aches and pains and feels that the massage is really helping. As this was her last treatment, I wanted to use one of the more expensive oils to 'pamper' her. We tested Rose damask, Neroli and Jasmine. Mrs CD preferred Rose damask so I incorporated it into the blend. Proposed treatment to uplift, relax, and aid stress symptoms.

Rationale for the choice of each essence

Basil (Lamiaceae, Ocimum basilicum, Alcohols) – Antidepressant, cephalic, nervine, muscular aches and pains
Bergamot (Rutaceae, Citrus bergamia, Esters) – Antidepressant, uplifting, relaxing, strengthens immune system
Rose damask (Rosaceae, Rosa damascena, Alcohols) – Antidepressant, relaxing, sedative, tonic

Rationale for choice of each fixed oil

Almond Oil was chosen for its nourishing properties and it has been readily absorbed by Mrs CD's skin in previous treatments. Jojoba was chosen for the face, as she did not like Almond oil used last week.

Alternative oils

Jasmine – Relaxing, sedative, tonic
Neroli – Antidepressant, antispasmodic, relaxing, sedative, tonic, uplifting
Cedarwood Atlas – Sedative
Petitgrain – Antidepressant, sedative
Cypress – Menopausal symptoms, tonic

Ratio of blending

Body
20ml Almond Oil
2 drops – Basil
4 drops – Bergamot (bergaptene free)
1 drop – Rose damask

Face
5 ml Jojoba – Mimics sebum, easily absorbed by skin
1 drop – Rose damask

Client Feedback

She said that she felt really good and her energy levels had remained 'up' all evening after the last treatment. This continued for a couple of days but that she had experienced occasional 'down' moments this week. She quickly relaxed and actually fell asleep during this treatment. It was a surprise as I had chosen oils to uplift her!

After the treatment, she said that she had particularly enjoyed the Rose damask oil when it was used on her face. She also said that she felt 'like a weight had been lifted' from her and she felt relaxed but not sleepy.

Aftercare/home care advice

She had a glass of water and visited the toilet. Mrs CD was reminded of the general aftercare. She could increase her use of oils now to reinforce any professional treatments and I gave her a list of suitable oils with suggestions for the most beneficial. I recommended that she continue with aromatherapy massage at least once per month to help with her stress levels and general relaxation. I put the remainder of the facial oil into a bottle for her to take home and reapply nightly.

Self Reflection

I felt that this treatment was successful. I did not want to sedate her but to help her gently relax and I think the blend chosen did that. It was her favourite of the blends used over the last four weeks, and seemed to lift her spirits almost immediately. I used Jojoba but found it too sticky on the face and will continue to use Evening primrose in future for this client. Almond oil was suitable for the body, but Mrs CD does not like the feel of it on her face. I concentrated treating Mrs CD's stress symptoms but many of the oils chosen were suitable for muscular aches, pains and the nervous system as well as menopausal symptoms. The massage routine I used consisted mainly of effleurage and lymphatic drainage movements, which seemed to calm the client. My pressure point techniques have improved; I am more accurate in my placement and confident of applying a suitable pressure for the client. I have also learned to be sensitive to areas of tension when applying pressure, as it can be uncomfortable for the client. I concentrated on using uplifting oils overall rather than heavily sedative oils to try to achieve balance. I am glad to have had the opportunity to work with someone who has serious health issues – it was good experience and I felt that I did help to balance her moods and energy levels through the use of the oils, massage and my home care recommendations.

Conclusion

Considering her condition, she is in relatively good health at the moment. She needs to be careful not to overwork and burn out. She should take up an activity like yoga or pilates to help keep her body supple and prevent aches and pains. She could also try meditation or breathing exercises to help lower her stress levels.

CPD Requirements

This was a very interesting case study to work on. I need to gain more knowledge about the menopause and its effects and to this end I have booked myself onto a weekend course specifically designed for tailoring aromatherapy treatments for this particular client group.

Alphabetical list of diseases and disorders for consideration during consultation for Aromatherapy

Acne Vulgaris
Addison's Disease
Acquired Immune-deficiency Syndrome (AIDS)
Alcohol
Allergic reactions / Allergies to essences / fixed carrier oils
Amenorrhoea
Anaemia
Ankle tendon injuries
Ankylosing spondylitis
Angina
Aneurysm
Asthma
Athlete's foot
Autoimmune diseases
Bells Palsy
Boils and carbuncles
Blisters
Bronchitis
Bruising
Bursitis
Calf pain
Cancer (skin, prostate, benign tumours, lung)
Carpal Tunnel Syndrome
Cirrhosis of the liver
Colitis
Crohn's disease
Cushings syndrome
Deep Vein Thrombosis (DVT)
Deltoid Bursitis
Diabetes
Discharge from a vaginal infection
Diverticulitis
Drugs
Dysmenorrhoea
Embolism
Emphysema
Endometriosis

Epilepsy
Fractures (partial, simple, compound)
Fibrosis
Fibromyalgia
Fibrositis and muscular rheumatism
Follicultis
Frozen shoulder
Gallstones
Goitre
Gout
Grave's disease
Haemophilia
Heart attack / Heart failure / Stroke
Heart Burn or indigestion
Osteoporosis
Haematoma
Hepatitis
Herpes
Hiatus Hernia
High Blood pressure / Hypertension
Housemaid's knee
Hormonal implants
Hypothyroidism / Hyperthyroidism
Impetigo
Influenza
Kidney stones
Laryngitis
Leukaemia
Low blood pressure / Hypotension
Lumbago
Lymphoedema
Meningitis
Menstruation
Menopause
Menorrhagia
Methicillin-resistant Staphylococcus aureus (MRSA)

Migraines / severe headaches
Motor Neurone Disease
Multiple sclerosis
Muscle overuse
Muscular dystrophy
Myalgic encephalitis (ME)
Myasthenia gravis
Nausea
Neuralgia
Neuritis
Oedema
Osteoarthritis
Osteomalacia
Osteoporosis
Paget's disease
Parasites
Parkinson's disease
Pediculosis (capitis, corporis, pubis)
Pelvic inflammatory infection
Phlebitis
Pins and needles or numbness
Pineal / Pituitary imbalance
Pleurisy
Pneumonia
Pregnancy
Prolapsed uterus / vagina
Polycystic Ovarian Syndrome
Psoriasis
Renal failure
Repetitive strain injury (RSI)
Respiratory disorders
Ringworm
Rheumatoid Arthritis
Scabies
Sciatica
Seasonal affective disorder (SAD)

Severe trauma
Sexually Transmitted Diseases (STD)
Shin splints
Shingles
Sickle cell anaemia
Sinusitis
Skin tags
Slipped disc (herniated disc)
Spasms / cramps
Spinal curvature
Sprains
Strain
Stomach / duodenum Ulcer
Stretch marks
Tendonitis
Tennis elbow, golfers elbow
Tinea corporis / Tinea Pedis
Thickening of the arteries
Thin skin
Thrombosis
Transient Ischaemic Attack (TIA)
Trigeminal neuralgia
Tuberculosis (TB)
Urinary tract infections
Unexplained lumps
Varicose veins
Verrucae
Warts
Whiplash

Bibliography

- Arnould-Taylor, WE, *Aromatherapy for the Whole Person* (Leckhampton: Stanley Thornes, 1981)

- Davis, Patricia, *Aromatherapy: an A-Z* (Saffron Walden: C.W.Daniel, 1999)

- Lawless, Julia, *The Encyclopaedia of Essential Oils* (Shaftesbury: Element, 1992; reprinted 2000)

- Maxwell-Hudson, Clare, *The Complete Book of Massage* (London: Dorling Kindersley, 1988)

- Price, Shirley, *The Aromatherapy Workbook* (London: Thorsons, 1998)

- Price, Shirley and Len, *Aromatherapy for Health Professionals* (Edinburgh: Churchill Livingstone, 1995)

- Room, Adrian (Ed), *Brewer's Dictionary of Phrase and Fable*, 15th edition (London: Cassell, 1997)

Glossary

Absolute: thick liquid made from blending concrete with alcohol, then removing alcohol by evaporation

Acupuncture: Chinese technique involving the insertion of needles into energy points of the body

Adulterate: change the purity (and thus the effectiveness) of an essential oil by various methods of dilution and substitution

Aromatherapy: the use of essential oils and plant essences in therapeutic treatments

Aromatic: having a smell, or fragrance

Atom: the tiniest particle of matter

Avicenna: credited with developing/inventing distillation technique for extracting oils

Ayurvedic medicine: traditional Indian herbal medicine

Carrier oil: an oil from a plant, flower, nut or seed, used in blend with essential oils for treatments. Carrier can also be creams, gels or shampoos

Chemotype: a plant that is botanically identical to another (two rose bushes for example) but chemically different because it has been grown in different conditions (different geographical place, altitude, climate, cultivation)

Concrete: waxy residue containing plant essence that is obtained through solvent extraction

Desquamation: the flaking-off of dead skin cells

Elasticity: the ability to stretch

Element: the purest state of a chemical component

Essence: a plant's oil (not yet extracted or extracted by expression)

Essential oil: a plant's essence (that has been extracted by distillation)

Gattefossé, René Maurice: French scientist who reintroduced the use of essential oils in complementary therapy to the Western world and invented the term 'aromathérapie'

Herbal: a book on the subject of herb/plant properties, uses and benefits (common in 18th and 19th centuries)

Hippocrates: 'father of medicine'; greatly added to and developed knowledge and use of plants and herbs in medical remedies

Holistic: addressing the whole, not just a part

Hydrocarbon: a molecule made of hydrogen and carbon atoms

Hydrolat: aromatic or scented water, often the by-product of distillation

Inorganic: non-living

Integral: concerning the whole, not just a part

Maury, Marguerite: Austrian biochemist who brought aromatherapy to Britain

Molecule: a group of atoms joined together

'Nature-identical': synthetic oils that contain some organic molecules from cheap essential oils

Organic: living

Oxygenated compound: a molecule made of hydrogen, carbon and oxygen atoms

Percolation: distillation process that uses steam but pushes steam down through the plant material instead of up

Pharmacological: a chemical effect

Photosynthesis: the process by which a plant captures the energy of the sun, via a pigment in its leaves called chlorophyll, and uses it to convert carbon dioxide into organic substances

Phototoxicity: skin is sensitive to and possibly damaged by sunlight

Physiological: a physical effect

Pomade: fatty solid containing plant essence that is obtained through enfleurage

Psychological: an effect on the mind

Shiatsu: Chinese technique using the same energy points as acupuncture but applying finger and thumb pressure to them instead of using needles

Solvent extraction: use of a chemical substance to extract plant essence

Stable: will not evaporate in air

Still: the equipment used to extract plant essences by distillation: consists of vessel for holding plant material, pipes to transfer steam, condenser, heat source

Synergy: how all the different molecules of an oil combine and work together as a whole oil, producing different effects to those of each molecule group used individually

Trace element: a tiny amount of an element

Valnet, Jean: French doctor who continued the work of Gattefossé

Volatile: will evaporate in air

GLOSSARY

Index

DON'T FORGET TO
USE YOUR RESOURCE
CD ROM

**TEST YOUR
KNOWLEDGE OF
ESSENTIAL OILS**

**TEST YOUR
KNOWLEDGE
QUESTIONS**

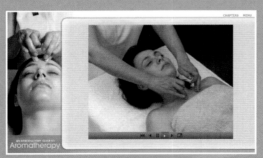

**FULL VIDEO OF
PRACTICAL SKILLS**

AND MUCH MORE!

An introductory guide
to Aromatherapy